The
BIG BOOK
of
WORLD WAR II

by Melissa Wagner and Dan Bryant

RP|CLASSICS
PHILADELPHIA • LONDON

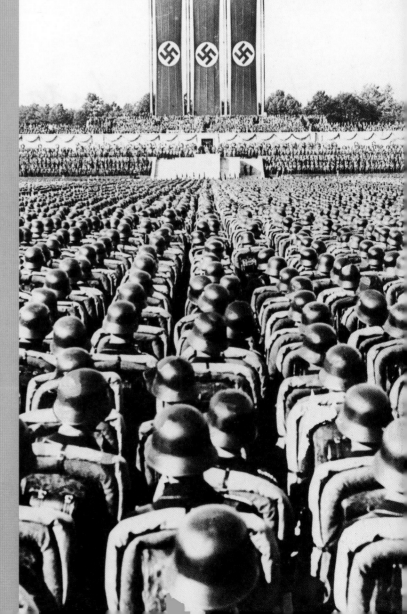

© 2009 by Running Press Classics

All rights reserved under the Pan-American and
International Copyright Conventions

Printed in China

9   8   7   6   5   4   3   2   1
Digit on the right indicates the number of this printing.

Library of Congress Control Number: 2008933268

Cover design by Ryan Hayes
Interior design by 21xdesign.com
Edited by Kelli Chipponeri
Typography: Arno Pro and Gill Sans

Published by Running Press Classics, an imprint of
Running Press Book Publishers
2300 Chestnut Street
Philadelphia, PA 19103-4371

Visit us on the web!
www.runningpress.com

Previous page: Men of the 45th division of the U.S. 7th Army wave American flags
from the dais of the Luitpold Arena in Nuremberg after capturing the city. It was in this
very arena that the annual Nazi party rallies were held. April 1945

This page: Massed troops stand at attention and listen to speeches during a Nazi rally
in Nuremberg, Germany, September 1934. Among the speakers at the rally were the
Austrian-born leader of the Nazi Party Adolf Hitler (1889–1945) and German-born
party spokesman Joseph Goebbels (1897–1945).

Opposite (top): Bomber crews of the U.S. Ninth Air force leave their B26 Marauder
aircraft after returning from a mission to support the D-Day landings in Normandy by
disrupting German lines of communication and supply. June 7, 1944

Opposite (bottom): Flag raising on Iwo Jima. February 23, 1945

Table of Contents

The World Before the War

EUROPE, 1919 - 1929
The National Boundary Realignments Resulting From the First World War

The seeds of World War II were planted by the victors at the end of World War I, a devastating conflict that had torn Europe apart between 1914 and 1918. The First World War had been a battle between the Central Powers, namely Germany, Austria-Hungary, and Turkey, against the Allied Powers of France, Great Britain, the United States, Russia, Italy, and Japan. In the end, the Allies were victorious, but millions of soldiers and civilians from both sides had been killed or injured during WWI, and even the victorious European countries were left with bombed-out cities and populations suffering from poverty and disease.

1. National Boundary Realignments from the First World War, Europe. 1919–1929
2. Poor German women sift through garbage looking for food in post war Germany. 1918
3. Children at a street kitchen. December 17, 1918
4. Old railway carriages are used to house whole families during Germany's post-war economic crisis.
5. Thomas Woodrow Wilson, twenty-eighth President of the United States.

At the Paris Peace Conference in the spring of 1919, leaders from the Allied governments met to draft a treaty that would mark the official end of WWI. None of the defeated countries had any input in the agreement, and though representatives of all the Allies were in attendance, most of the decisions were made by the leaders from France, Great Britain, and the U.S. These Allied nations blamed Germany for the war, and they wanted Germany to pay.

When the German delegation was presented with a finished treaty, they were surprised at how severely the Allies wanted to punish them. They felt the treaty did not properly represent the terms of the truce they agreed to when they stopped fighting months earlier. Though they disagreed with the proposed treaty, they were forced to sign it despite their protests.

The agreement, called the Treaty of Versailles, carved up the German and Austro-Hungarian empires, changing the borders of many of the countries of Europe and reducing the population and territory of Germany by about 10 percent. Some people whose homes were in Germany before the treaty found themselves living in Austria, Czechoslovakia, Poland, Denmark, Belgium, or France after the agreement was signed. The treaty limited the number of soldiers in the German army, forbade Germany from manufacturing military vehicles like tanks and submarines, and restricted the number of German factories that could make weapons. But from Germany's perspective, the worst part of the treaty was the "war guilt clause," which laid all the blame for the war on Germany and made its citizens responsible for paying the Allied nations for damages they suffered as a result of the war. The German people felt it was unfair to blame their country for the whole war and to force

June 28, 1919:
The Treaty of Versailles is signed, formalizing the end of World War I. Germany is forced to accept economically crippling terms.

British Prime Minister Lloyd George signing the Treaty of Versailles. France. June 28, 1919

February 24, 1920:
The German Workers' Party changes its name to The National Socialist German Workers' Party (the Nazi Party).

October 31, 1922:
Fascist Benito Mussolini takes power in Italy.

them to pay to rebuild the rest of Europe, when they themselves had their own rebuilding to do.

Other countries were also unhappy with the treaty. Italy believed it had been neglected when Germany's territories were being divided. Japan felt that it had been ignored during the negotiations because of the Allied nations' racial prejudice. Even the U.S., which had been instrumental in the creation of the treaty, was not happy—so much so that the U.S. Senate refused to ratify (approve) it. One point of contention was the formation of a League of Nations. This would be a world governing body whose members agreed to recognize and protect one another's independence and national borders. Some U.S. Senators did not want to be involved in more European disputes, especially since the high cost of WWI was so much on their minds.

During the 1920s, Europe struggled to recover from the destruction of the war. Some countries, including the Soviet Union, France, Austria, Hungary, and Germany, experienced severe inflation that made

prices soar to shocking levels. This was especially difficult for the German middle class, whose life savings became worthless overnight. Germany worked together with other European countries and the U.S. to restore some value to their currency, but the German masses, regardless of class, suffered throughout the 1920s.

Then another economic disaster struck. In October 1929, the U.S. stock market crashed and investors lost everything. Around the world, banks failed, companies went bankrupt, and millions were put out of work. The 1930s were the time of the Great Depression; jobs were hard to come by, and it seemed everyone was poor and desperate. Countries stopped working with one another, and international trade slowed down.

Germany was once again struck particularly hard. For the second time in a decade, the German economy was on the verge of collapse. The German people were desperate for a way out of this crisis. They looked for a new leader who could restore order and help them back to their feet. ✪

THE LEAGUE OF NATIONS

As a part of the Treaty of Versailles, U.S. President Woodrow Wilson championed the formation of a League of Nations to help countries work together to prevent war. The League would be a place for disputing countries to discuss their problems. The League would listen and recommend a peaceful course of action. If one of the countries continued to threaten the peace, the League could impose economic sanctions, where other member nations would refuse to trade with that country. If that didn't work, the League could threaten physical force, but the League had no army or soldiers of its own to back up its threats. If none of the member nations sent an army to fight, then there would be no way of carrying out the threat. Though the League was not a success because several principal nations, including the U.S., refused to join, it did provide the basis for the United Nations, which was formed after World War II and took on much of the League's purpose, methods, and structure.

January 30, 1933:
Under pressure, Germany's president, Paul von Hindenburg, appoints Hitler to the position of chancellor, the chief government executive.

Adolf Hitler (right), poses with Paul von Hindenburg, 85, German general and President, after his appointment as Chancellor of Germany. Berlin, Germany. January 30, 1933

August 2, 1934:
Hindenburg dies; seventeen days later Hitler officially becomes *der führer* (the Leader), assuming the role of both chancellor and president.

September 1935:
The swastika flag becomes the lone national flag of Germany.

Hitler and the Third Reich

As the head of the Nazi Party (short for National Socialist German Workers' Party), Adolf Hitler presented himself as a leader with ideas that could end the hardships Germans were experiencing. Hitler promised to reject the oppressive Treaty of Versailles, recover economic strength, and eventually take a place at the head of the world. He and the Nazis believed that the Aryans, people of Teutonic and Nordic descent, or "pure" Germans, were members of a master race. Hitler claimed that Jews were behind all the negative things that had happened to Germany; that Jews controlled Germany's international enemies, such as the Allied victors of WWI; and that if Germany was rid of its ethnic minorities, especially those of Jewish descent, then Germany's problems would disappear.

1. Adolf Hitler and Benito Mussolini in Munich, Germany. ca. June 1940.
2. Hitler accepts the ovation of the Reichstag after announcing the "peaceful" acquisition of Austria. It set the stage to annex the Czechoslovakian Sudetenland, largely inhabited by a German-speaking population. Berlin. March 1938.
3. Adolf Hitler (right), wearing a swastika armband, shakes hands with British Prime Minister Neville Chamberlain during their meeting at the Hotel Dreesen at Godesberg. September 23, 1938

Many voters are impressed by Hitler's promises and by the end of 1932, the Nazi Party held more seats in the Reichstag, the German parliament, than any other party. On January 30, 1933, Germany's president, General Paul von Hindenburg, appointed Hitler the chancellor (the chief minister of the government). On March 23, 1933, the Reichstag passed a law that enabled Hitler's government to bypass the German constitution and make laws without seeking the approval of the Reichstag or the president. Hitler had been made a dictator, a leader with absolute power.

Hitler wasted no time in putting his plans for Germany in motion. He had a special police force made up of Nazi extremists and put them to work to secure his ambitions. Hitler disbanded all trade unions, outlawed all non-Nazi political parties, and had his special police arrest anyone he considered threatening or undesirable, including Jews, Gypsies, intellectuals, the handicapped, and priests, among others. None of the people were given a fair trial. Instead they were shipped to prison camps where many were tortured and killed.

After President Hindenburg died in 1934, Hitler took on the role of president as well. He called his regime the Third Reich, or third empire, continuing a tradition of strong German states, and he secretly told his generals to prepare for war. German engineers worked on designs for new and powerful tanks, submarines, and weapons. In March 1935, he took a bold step in making public his rebellion against the Treaty of Versailles. Hitler announced the creation of a German air force, the Luftwaffe, and called for the recruitment of thousands of men for the German army. Hitler's announcement also included plans for a greatly expanded naval force. By 1939, German troop levels had reached 4.5 million. A year later, in direct opposition to the treaty, he sent troops into the Rhineland, the area of Germany that borders France, Belgium, and the Netherlands. Though the treaty specifically stated that the German military was subject to force if it entered the Rhineland, the rest of the world did nothing to stop the incoming troops.

September 15, 1935:
The Nuremberg Laws are passed, which deny German Jews of many of their civil rights.

Jews from the Warsaw ghetto surrender to German soldiers after the uprising.

October 3, 1935:
Italy invades Ethiopia (also called Abyssinia).

March 7, 1936:
Hitler violates the Treaty of Versailles by sending his army into the Rhineland on Germany's western border, which bordered France. Britain and Italy do nothing, despite their guarantee to defend the territory.

OPPOSING POLITICAL PHILOSOPHIES

In a democracy, the power rests with the citizens, who elect representatives to speak for them in a governing body. In the 1930s and '40s, the United States, Great Britain, France, Belgium, Iceland, the Netherlands, and Sweden were among the countries with some form of democratic government.

In a fascist state, country and race are more important than one individual person. The government is led by a dictator who exacts strict control over the freedom of the people, usually by using brute force to discourage opposing political beliefs. Germany, Italy, Japan, and Spain were all countries with fascist governments in the lead-up to World War II.

Communists believe in a society in which all land, businesses, and material goods are owned by the community as a whole and distributed to individuals as needed, with the goal of destroying all social classes. The Soviet Union was the only country claiming communist rule before WWII, but in reality its leader, Joseph Stalin, behaved more like a fascist dictator than a true communist leader.

> ### "I believe it is peace in our time."
> —*Neville Chamberlain*

Meanwhile, those labeled Jews were stripped of their German citizenship, and marriage between Jews and those labeled Germans was forbidden. Jews were no longer allowed to work for the government or in universities, and Jewish businesses were boycotted. But even as the Jews were being persecuted, other Germans felt like the country's luck had turned. Partly because of the focus on military equipment and weaponry, many Germans were working and enjoying financial stability again.

In March 1938, Hitler made a dramatic move. He sent German troops into Austria to take over the country in the Anschluss ("joining together" or "connection"). Though many Austrians were in favor of the unification of the countries (many Austrians were of German descent and Hitler was, in fact, Austrian), this was an obvious violation of the Treaty of Versailles. The Nazis began to round up Jews in both Germany and Austria and forced them to live in small, cramped areas of the cities called ghettos.

After success in Austria, Hitler sized up Czechoslovakia. Hitler desired an area called the Sudetenland, but Czechoslovakia didn't intend to let it go without a fight. The Czechs called on other European nations to help them convince Hitler to stop his plans. Hitler vowed that if the Czechs didn't hand over the Sudetenland, then the Nazis would take the whole country by force.

To settle the matter, representatives of Germany, Britain, France, and Italy met in Munich on September 29, 1938. Czechoslovakia was excluded from the conversation that would seal its fate. In order to keep the peace, the parties agreed to transfer the Sudetenland to Germany in return for Hitler's promise to resolve future differences through consultation rather than war. Czechoslovakia reluctantly went along with the agreement, for without military support from France and Britain they would be unable to defend themselves. Britain's prime minister Neville Chamberlain, was jubilant, announcing that the Munich Agreement represented "peace with honor."

Just five months later, Hitler ignored the Munich Agreement, and his troops invaded the remainder of Czechoslovakia for the Reich. ⊙

4. *Daily Herald* shows the famous headline "Peace For Our Time" after British Prime Minister Neville Chamberlain had returned from his Munich talks with Adolf Hitler. October 1, 1938

5. Nazi staff cars enter a Sudetenland village to an enthusiastic reception, complete with Nazi salutes, from the local residents after occupation of the area by German troops.

November 25, 1936:
Germany and Japan sign a pact against Communism.

Yosuke Matsuoka, the Japanese Foreign Minister, with the German dictator Adolf Hitler at the Chancellory in Berlin. April 11, 1941

July 7, 1937:
Japan commences a full-scale invasion of China. Invasion begins with the so-called Marco Polo Bridge Incident.

March 12, 1938:
German troops march into Austria; many Austrians welcome the unification of the two countries.

Blitzkrieg!

As he had done with Czechoslovakia, Hitler pressured Poland to give up what he felt rightfully belonged to Germany. This time, the territory in question was the Polish Corridor, a strip of land leading to the Baltic Sea that had been given to Poland in the Treaty of Versailles. Poland refused Hitler's demands, and it began to prepare for war. France and England vowed they would come to Poland's aid if Germany invaded.

1. An anti-aircraft gun protects pioneer troops building a temporary bridge to help the advancing German troops. September 1939

2. This woman is unable to conceal her feelings as she salutes Hitler.

3. German troops parade in front of Adolf Hitler and Nazi Generals after entry into Warsaw. October 5, 1939

4. German Aggressions, Europe. 1936–1939

5. As a part of the wartime evacuation of London, parents escort their children to trains that will take them to the country and seaside for the duration of the combat. London, England. 1941

On August 23, 1939, the Germans and Soviets surprised the world by signing the Nazi-Soviet Pact, a formal agreement in which they promised not to attack each other. Because of the different political beliefs of the fascist Germans and the communist Soviets and their history of conflict during WWI, the two nations were natural enemies. In fact, just months before, the Soviet Union had tried to convince the Western powers to wage war on Germany. This strange Nazi-Soviet friendship could be partially explained by both powers' desire to expand into Polish territory. Unknown to the rest of the world, a secret section of the agreement divided the countries of Eastern Europe between Germany and the Soviet Union. Each agreed to divide Poland, and the Soviets would be free to invade Latvia, Estonia, and Finland without German interference. With the signing of the pact, Poland's fate was sealed.

At approximately 4:45 a.m. on September 1, 1939, the German army invaded Poland and introduced the world to a brutally effective new form of attack called *blitzkrieg*, or "lightning war." Unlike the stationary, trench-based warfare of World War I, blitzkrieg was fast and highly mobile. In a strategy that the Nazi forces repeated again and again in the years to come, they rolled hundreds of their tanks and military vehicles across the Polish border. Then followed thousands of infantry (foot soldiers) and artillery (large, heavy guns). As the ground forces drove forward, the German air force, the Luftwaffe, attacked and destroyed airfields full of fighter planes, crucial sections of the railways, and other strategic military targets before assisting the ground attack.

Two German army groups simultaneously attacked toward the Polish capital of Warsaw from different directions, with the ultimate goal of encircling the Polish army and forcing surrender. The Poles fought hard, and though they had the fifth-largest army in Europe at the time, much of their equipment was out-dated, and they weren't prepared to defend against Hitler's new form of warfare.

On September 3, 1939, Great Britain and France declared war on Germany, followed by many of Britain's current and former colonies, including Canada, Australia, India, South Africa, and Rhodesia (now called Zimbabwe). However, by then the Nazis' plan to surround the Polish army was already well under way, and Polish soldiers were being forced to surrender as the Nazis closed in on Warsaw. On September 17, the Polish government left the country in exile. The Polish ambassador in Moscow received a note from the Soviets telling him that his country no longer existed. By the end of the month, all of Poland

September 29–30, 1938: European leaders meet in Munich in response to Hitler's desire to extend Germany's reach into the Sudetenland in Czechoslovakia.

October 1, 1938: The German army invades the Sudetenland.

November 9–10, 1938: Nazi police and citizens terrorize German and Austrian Jews on *Kristallnacht* (Night of Broken Glass), a night on which ninety-one Jews were killed and 30,000 Jewish men were arrested and taken to concentration camps.

A worker clears broken glass of a Jewish shop following the anti-Jewish riots of Kristallnacht in Berlin.

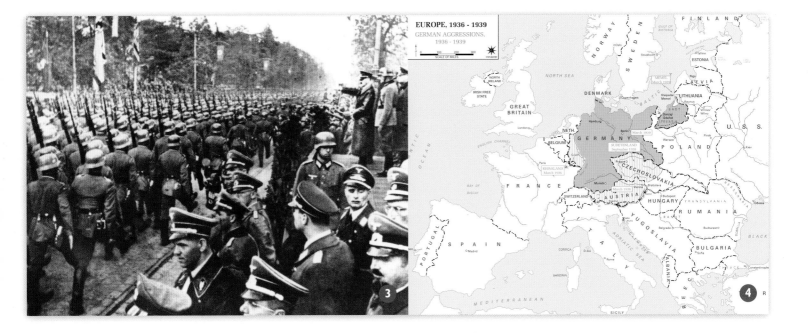

had fallen, with the Nazis and the Soviets splitting the country in two.

That October, as per the secret agreement in the Nazi-Soviet Pact, the Soviets established bases in the Baltic countries of Lithuania, Latvia, and Estonia and were occupying these nations by June 1940. The Soviet Army also invaded the Scandinavian country of Finland on November 30, 1939 and engaged in a brutal winter battle that lasted four months until the Finns surrendered the territory the Soviets demanded.

Hitler also wanted to acquire Scandinavian territory. He needed more seaports closer to the British Isles in order to stage an effective battle against the powerful British and French navies. On April 9, 1940, German armies invaded Denmark and Norway. Denmark surrendered without much of a fight. Some Danish army troops countered the invasion, but the government surrendered within two hours of the invasion. The Danish navy didn't fire a single shot at the invading forces. The Norwegians mounted a brave defense. Britain and France sent troops to help the Norwegians, but when Hitler attacked France in June, the Allies turned all their attention to the European mainland and Norway fell to the Germans. ✪

THE PHONY WAR

The citizens of Great Britain and France initially panicked when their countries declared war against Germany. In Great Britain, defensive preparations were quickly undertaken. Men were called to military service, bomb shelters were constructed, gas masks were distributed, volunteers were recruited for war-related civic duties, cities were kept dark at night, and food was rationed. Because of the fear of air raids in the cities, millions of British schoolchildren boarded trains bound for the countryside. They left behind their parents and school friends to move in with strangers in safer rural locations. Yet after the initial rush of preparation, nothing seemed to happen. Months went by without any land-based fighting between the Allies and the Nazis. Over time, the public's attitude about the war changed from fear to boredom. This period is often called the "Phony War" or the "Bore War" (Germans labeled it "Sitzkrieg") and lasted from September 1939 to late spring 1940.

May 22, 1939:
Italy and Germany sign the Pact of Steel, agreeing to fight side by side in any military conflict.

August 23, 1939:
Germany and the Soviets sign an agreement not to fight each other and to divide Poland.

September 1, 1939:
Germany invades Poland, prompting the official beginning of World War II.

The front page of London's *Evening Standard*, announcing the German invasion of Poland at the start of World War II. September 1, 1939

The Fall of Frances and the Low Countries

The small countries of Belgium, Luxembourg, and the Netherlands decided not to take sides in the fight with Hitler in hopes they could avoid war. But Hitler had other plans. He would attack across the continent and extend his empire all the way across Europe to the Atlantic Ocean.

On May 10, 1940, the Germans' westward invasion arrived. The Nazis made a blitzkrieg attack on Belgium, Luxembourg, and the Netherlands, all of which lacked the support of in-country Allied troops due to their neutrality. After their swift assault of the Low Countries, German troops pushed south through France's northern border. The Nazis also surprised the Allies by staging a massive, successful charge into France through the barely guarded Ardennes, a hilly, thickly forested region near France's border with Luxembourg and Belgium. The French assumed the area was safe because they thought the landscape would be impossible for German tanks to drive through.

The German army's surge drove a wedge between the various factions of the Allied forces, trapping 380,000 people, including British soldiers and Frenchmen at the town of Dunkirk on the coast of the English Channel. Just when it seemed as though many of the Allies' best soldiers would be forced to surrender, Hitler made a tactical error. He ordered his ground troops to hold off on attacking Dunkirk to allow the Luftwaffe to finish off the Allies with an air bombardment. Hermann Goering, the head of the Luftwaffe and one of Hitler's closest advisors, had assured him that the Luftwaffe could do the job alone. But the British Royal Air Force (RAF) fought doggedly, allowing for the cross-Channel

evacuation of 338,000 troops in what British Prime Minister Winston Churchill called the "Miracle at Dunkirk." Veteran soldiers as well as ordinary English farmers, salesmen, civil servants, and factory workers manned virtually any craft that would float. This included naval and merchant marine vessels, civilian yachts, and even small fishing boats. They carried Allied soldiers to large British ships waiting offshore. Though the Germans killed, wounded, or captured more than 68,000 Allied troops at Dunkirk, the effort of the British Navy, the RAF, and the civilian volunteers saved the army.

Meanwhile, German Field Marshal Karl Rudolf Gerd von Rundstedt regrouped his army for an assault to the south. The French had already lost many of their best troops in Belgium, and though they mounted a defense at the Somme and Aisne rivers, the Germans easily pushed through the line on June 5. By June 12, Paris was abandoned, and the Germans marched in on June 14. A week later, French Marshal Philippe Pétain signed a formal surrender on behalf of France. To humiliate the French, the Nazis re-created a scene from the end of World War I, insisting that Pétain sign the paperwork in the same railway car in which the Germans had been forced to surrender to the Allies two decades earlier.

The defeated country was divided into two sections. Nazi soldiers occupied northern France

September 3, 1939:
Britain and France declare war on Germany.

April 9, 1940:
Germany attacks Norway and Denmark. Denmark surrenders; Allied troops arrive to support the Norwegians, but are forced to retreat.

May 10, 1940:
Hitler invades the Low Countries of Belgium, Luxembourg, and the Netherlands. The German invasion of France begins the same day.

AMERICAN ISOLATIONISM

In the early years of Hitler's conquests in Europe, many Americans wanted to remain uninvolved in the conflict. These Americans, called isolationists, wanted the U.S. to focus on improving the situation at home, ignoring the affairs of the rest of the world. Americans had suffered terribly through the years of the Great Depression, and though President Roosevelt's New Deal policies helped the American economy, people felt there was still much to be done. They were mindful of the sacrifices American soldiers made in Europe during World War I, and the new European war seemed to have little to do with them.

But President Franklin Roosevelt could see that the Axis powers would not be satisfied until they dominated the world; he knew that the U.S. would be pulled into the war eventually. He was concerned that the U.S. military was not prepared. Although Congress and the isolationists initially opposed his ideas to spend tax money on modernizing and strengthening the army, they agreed to support a buildup after the fall of France. Roosevelt encouraged U.S. industry to manufacture weapons and war vehicles. He hoped that America could provide Britain and France with equipment and supplies needed to keep the Allies fighting without the help of U.S. soldiers.

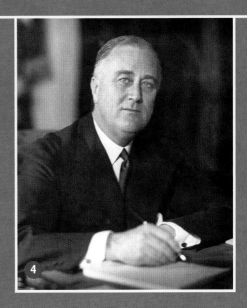

under Hitler's rule, and southern France, which came to be known as "Vichy France," was to be governed by Pétain from the city of Vichy. However, Pétain's government was a "puppet" government, or a government under the control of another country—in this case, Germany and Hitler.

Throughout the war, many French citizens refused to submit to German rule. A group called the French Forces of the Interior continued fighting the Germans from within France and another group, led by General Charles de Gaulle, set up a new French government in exile in London. This group, called the Free French, still had the remnants of the trained French army who had not been captured, and they joined the Allies in their continued fight against Germany. ✪

"... We shall go on to the end,
we shall fight in France, we shall fight
on the seas and oceans,
we shall fight with growing confidence
and growing strength in the air,
we shall defend our island, whatever
the cost may be, we shall fight on the
beaches, we shall fight on the
landing grounds, we shall fight
in the fields and in the streets,
we shall fight in the hills;
we shall never surrender..."

—*Winston Churchill, following the evacuation
of the Allied armies from Dunkirk*

1. General Charles de Gaulle inspects members of the newly formed Free French command unit at Wellington Barracks. ca. 1942
2. Der Fürer in Paris.
3. The Arc de Triomphe is visible behind german troops as they ride down a street in occupied Paris.
4. Franklin Roosevelt, thirty-second President of the United States.
5. The Pursuit, Western Europe. 1940

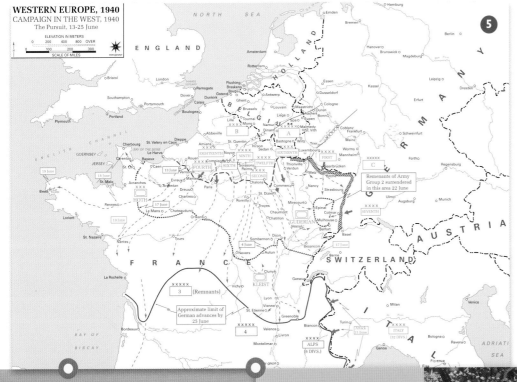

WESTERN EUROPE, 1940
CAMPAIGN IN THE WEST, 1940
The Pursuit, 13-25 June

May 10, 1940:
Winston Churchill becomes prime minister of Great Britain.

May 26, 1940:
Allies launch Operation Dynamo to evacuate British, French, and Belgian troops from the port town of Dunkirk, France.

Uniformed Allied soldiers stand on a ship during the evacuation of British and French troops from Dunkirk.

June 10, 1940:
Italy declares war on France and Britain, and invades an already weakened France eleven days later.

The Battle of Britain

Great Britain was next on Hitler's list. He went to the British and offered to make peace in turn for their recognition of the Nazi domination of Western Europe and a return of the colonies that had been taken from Germany in the Treaty of Versailles. Britain refused and prepared itself for a Nazi attack.

1. A Squadron of Spitfires takes off for a sweep over Holland, led by an Australian Wing Commander J. R. Ratten.
2. British Prime Minister Winston Churchill, the First Lord of the Admiralty, on his way to Downing Street on his 65th birthday. November 30, 1939
3. Londoners in a sandbag protected "Anderson" shelter. October 1941

Thus, on July 10, 1940, the Battle of Britain began when the Luftwaffe staged the first of many air raids on Britain. In the beginning, Germany's air force had the advantage in the fight, with more than three times as many total planes and twice as many bombers as the British. Hermann Goering, the head of the Luftwaffe, thought the Germans would destroy the British Royal Air Force in four days but he was wrong. The British Hurricane and Spitfire planes were well armed and highly maneuverable. They were a solid match for even the best of Germany's fighter planes, the Messerschmitt 109s. But the RAF had one distinct advantage—their use of radio detecting and ranging, or radar. In 1938, the British had installed the Chain Home, a string of radar stations along the English coast to detect incoming aircraft. Radar was still a relatively new technology at the time, and Goering never fully understood the advantage radar gave his Allied opponents. The Luftwaffe attacked these radar stations but concluded that they couldn't be destroyed from the air; they assaulted airfields and ports. But rather than focus on

one target and bomb it until it was destroyed, Goering employed a more scattershot method that allowed the British time to regroup, recover, and continue the fight.

As of September 7, 1940, the Nazis switched their tactics to focus more on civilian than military targets (London was bombed fifty-seven nights in a row, beginning on September 7). In a strategy designed to break the will of the British people, London and other major British cities became the primary focus for the Luftwaffe's air raids. Between September 1940 and May 1941, a period known as "the Blitz," the Luftwaffe made 127 large-scale night raids on Britain's cities, destroying approximately two million houses, injuring 139,000 British civilians, and killing 43,000.

But for all the damage the Luftwaffe inflicted on the ground, the RAF had the upper hand in the air. The Nazis realized that they would not be able to gain superiority over Britain in the air—the RAF was shooting down so many Luftwaffe planes that German factories couldn't make planes fast enough to keep up with the demand. Hitler postponed and eventually canceled the land invasion of Britain, and by the end of April 1941, the air raids stopped. The Battle of Britain was over, and the seemingly unbeatable Nazis had suffered defeat. ⊘

June 14, 1940:
The Nazis occupy Paris.

Adolf Hitler at the Eiffel Tower in Paris, with his generals during the German occupation of France. Also with him are sculptor Arno Breker (left) and architect Albert Speer (right). June 24, 1940

June 22, 1940:
France surrenders to Germany.

July 5, 1940:
The United States forbids American companies from shipping Japan any materials that could be used to help them at war.

WINSTON CHURCHILL

British Prime Minister Winston Churchill was one of the greatest heroes of World War II. He was a brave, outspoken, and inspirational leader whose buoyant spirit held Britain together during the worst years of the war.

Churchill led an extraordinary life. As a young man, he was both a soldier and journalist. He was appointed to Parliament in 1900, and was First Lord of the Admiralty during World War I, a position he held from October 1911 to May 1915, where he played an important role in Britain's war planning.

Though Churchill did not hold a cabinet position prior to WWII, he publicly spoke his mind about his concerns over Hitler's quest for power. He opposed Prime Minister Chamberlain's plan of appeasing Hitler to keep the peace. When war could no longer be avoided, Chamberlain appointed Churchill to his old post as First Lord of the Admiralty and to the War Cabinet. When Chamberlain resigned after Germany's invasion of Western Europe, Churchill was made prime minister.

As Britain's leader, Churchill formed a government that incorporated leaders from all political parties, unifying both the government and the people it led. His speeches inspired his people when Nazis were bombing British cities. Churchill's strength and persistence were important in the bond formed between the Allied nations of Britain, the Soviet Union, and the U.S.

"Never in the field of human conflict was so much owed by so many to so few."

—Winston Churchill, of the RAF fighters during the Battle of Britain

SHELTER FROM THE BOMBS

British citizens found cover from German bombs in several ways. Residents of houses with a backyard often constructed government-issued steel shelters, called Anderson Shelters. They were built partially underground and covered with dirt.

For people without backyards, the government developed a shelter that could be used indoors. Morrison Shelters were just large enough to sleep in and consisted of a thick rectangular steel frame, mesh sides, and a metal mesh "mattress" on the bottom that was designed to survive the impact of falling debris and keep its shape.

Large public shelters were built, but these quickly became unsanitary and overcrowded. As a result, many Londoners took refuge on the platforms of the subway system—the London Underground. At first the government discouraged this practice, but when it became clear that the people were going to use the stations no matter what, they installed special triple bunk beds, built additional toilets, established first aid clinics, and employed citizens as Shelter Marshals to help maintain order. At the peak of the air raids, approximately 175,000 people were sleeping in the stations officially approved for use as shelters. Even with all of these options for civilians, about two-thirds of Londoners remained in their homes during the air raids.

July 10, 1940:
The Battle of Britain begins.

September 7, 1940:
The Luftwaffe starts bombing civilian targets in Britain; London is bombed for the first of fifty-seven consecutive nights.

Coventry Cathedral in ruins after the night Blitz on Coventry. November 1940

September 13, 1940:
Italy attacks Egypt from Libya.

The Axis in the Mediterranean

While the Nazis concentrated on the Battle of Britain, their Axis partner, Italy, set out to expand their territory in another part of the world. Italian dictator Benito Mussolini had grand ambitions of creating a new Roman empire surrounding the Mediterranean Sea; he even referred to the Mediterranean as *mare nostrum* ("our sea"), just like the ancient Romans.

On September 13, 1940, a huge army of Italian troops based in Libya marched into Egypt in an attempt to capture the British-held Suez Canal, a strategically important channel that connects the Mediterranean Sea to the Red Sea. Though the Italian force was much larger than the Egypt-based British Army of the Nile, the Italians were ill-equipped and poorly trained for desert warfare. They initially charged several hundred miles into Egypt, but then they dug in at Sidi Barrani and didn't move for three months. In the meantime, the British built their strength, and despite the fact that they were still vastly outnumbered, the Brits attacked in December. By February 7, 1941, the British pushed the Italians halfway across Libya and captured more than 130,000 prisoners of war.

The Western Desert wasn't the only place the Italian army was facing defeat. On October 28, 1940, Italian forces in Albania had marched south into Greece, another key component in Mussolini's plan for Mediterranean domination. The Italians seemed to have the advantage because Greece didn't even have any tanks. But within three weeks, and with some help from the British RAF, the Greeks had not only pushed the Italians out of their country but they had also attacked Italian-held Albania.

Hitler couldn't allow Mussolini to give up so much territory in North Africa and the Mediterranean. In February 1941, he created the German Afrika Korps (*Deutches Afrikakorps*, in German) and appointed a young general, Erwin Rommel, to lead it. Rommel and his mighty tank divisions arrived in Libya in March and went on the offensive. They quickly recaptured the Libyan territory the British had taken from the Italians. By April 14, 1941, Rommel crossed into Egypt, where he was forced to stop due to dwindling supplies.

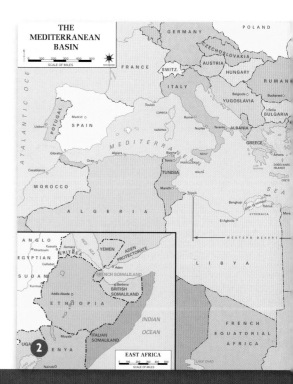

September 25, 1940:
American intelligence agents crack Japan's diplomatic code, known as "Purple."

September 27, 1940:
The Axis powers sign the Tripartite Pact, formalizing an economic and military alliance between Germany, Italy, and Japan.

October 28, 1940:
Italy invades Greece.

THE AXIS POWERS

Germany wasn't the only country with leaders set on using force to expand their power. In 1922, Benito Mussolini became prime minister and consolidated powers over the next three years, culminating with his assumption of the title *Il Duce*, or "supreme leader", in 1925. As the head of the fascist movement, he would not tolerate political differences. Mussolini promised to build on Italy's colonies in North Africa to form a new Italian empire. In October 1935, he ordered the invasion of Ethiopia.

There was trouble in the Far East as well. The island country of Japan was led by a militaristic government set on controlling all of Asia. Japan had a powerful navy and a large army. Japan wanted to secure the oil and other natural resources throughout South, East, and Southeast Asia, as well as the Pacific. In 1931, Japan invaded the Chinese province of Manchuria, and by 1937, the Japanese army had expanded the invasion to include China.

Hitler recognized he could benefit from forming an alliance with these nations. Germany, Italy, and Japan signed a series of pacts agreeing to work together. The three countries came to be known as the Axis powers. This term was created by Mussolini, who said that the line from Rome to Berlin was like an axis around which the rest of the world would turn.

The supply drain came because resources were being used in the German offensive back in Europe. On April 6, the Nazis waged a blitzkrieg attack on both Yugoslavia and Greece. Yugoslavia fell after just eleven days and Greece was under Nazi control by the end of the month. By mid-1941, with the exception of a couple of neutral countries, mainland Europe was under Axis rule. ✪

1. German paratroops land during the invasion of Crete.
2. The Mediterranean Basin, with an inset of East Africa.
3. Italian dictator Benito Mussolini on horseback. ca 1930
4. German troops raise swastika flags in the market place of Moudros in the Lemnos island, Greece. May 1941
5. General Erwin Rommel with the 15th Panzer Division between Tobruk and Sidi Omar. Sdf. Zwilling, Libya. 1941.

THE "DESERT FOX"

Erwin Rommel was one of Germany's most admired military leaders in World War II, respected for his bravery, tactical skill, and intelligence. Rommel began the war as leader in the battalion responsible for Hitler's personal safety. In 1940, he led a Panzer tank division in the invasion of France and proved himself to be a master of tank warfare. Hitler appointed him commander of the German Afrika Korps in 1941, and he quickly earned the nickname "Desert Fox" because of his successful assaults in the deserts of North Africa. Leading from the turret of a tank, he launched a series of successful surprise attacks against the British, though in the end, the Afrika Korps was too short on supplies and reinforcements to earn a victory.

After D-Day, Rommel realized that Germany could not win. He tried to convince Hitler to negotiate with the Allies for peace. On July 17, 1944, Rommel was injured when his car was forced off the road by machine-gun fire from a Royal Canadian Air Force fighter. As he recovered, Hitler became convinced that Rommel knew about an assassination plot against him. Hitler sent word that Rommel's family would be tortured unless he took his own life. On October 14, Rommel poisoned himself to save his family. Because he was a hero to the German people, the public was told that Rommel died from injuries sustained during the attack on his car. It wasn't until after the war that the truth about his death was released.

December 9, 1940:
British troops counterattack Italians in Egypt. The fighting lasts several weeks, but the British eventually force the Italians to retreat into Libya.

March 11, 1941:
President Roosevelt signs the Lend-Lease Act.

March 28, 1941:
A team of American physicists discovers plutonium-239, a uranium isotope required in the development of nuclear weapons.

The Battle of the Atlantic

The long, drawn-out struggle for control of the Atlantic Ocean may have been the most important battle of the war. As a small island nation, Great Britain relied on ships for its survival. Great Britain traded with other countries in order to maintain its global empire by importing supplies and raw materials. It also exported assembled goods to its soldiers and trading partners abroad. If its merchant ships were cut off from their access to the ocean, Britain would no longer be able to fight. When the war began, merchant ships began traveling in convoys, or groups, which were then escorted by warships for protection from Germany's stealthy U-boats (submarines) and warships.

At the start of the war, Germany had limited access to the open water. To gain the control in the ocean they needed to secure more Atlantic ports, their U-boats would need a shorter distance to travel for refueling. In April 1940, the Nazis invaded Norway and overtook its thousands of miles of coast access to the North Atlantic. Then they captured the ports of France and the Low Countries in June.

During this period, the German Admiral Karl Doenitz masterminded the "wolf pack" convoy attack technique, where several U-boats would lie in wait in a heavily trafficked shipping lane. When a convoy of foreign ships was located, typically at night, the U-boats would converge from all sides. This caused mass confusion and made it nearly impossible for the convoy guards to fight back. Thanks in large part to the U-boats, by the end of 1940, the British had lost more than 3.5 million tons of merchant shipping.

Toward the middle of 1941, Britain's luck began to turn. Due to British advances in intercepting and interpreting the Germans' coded communication and the equipping of Royal Navy escort ships with radar, the U-boats lost their greatest asset—the element of surprise. In addition, the United States helped out by getting more and more involved in the Atlantic battle in 1941. In March, Congress approved a bill that allowed President Roosevelt to send unlimited weapons and equipment to the Allies, including warships. Then, in spite of its official neutral stance in the war, the United States took over the defense of Iceland from the overtaxed British so they could focus their energies

April 6, 1941:
Germans attack Yugoslavia and Greece.

April 14, 1941:
After having regained the Libyan territory the Italians lost to the British, German General Erwin Rommel, nicknamed the "Desert Fox," and his Afrika Korps invade Egypt.

May 7, 1941:
The British find German secret code books and a code-writing machine.

German soldiers enciphering message in Nazi's secret Enigma code on machine in field.

closer to Europe. United States warships started escorting convoys across the Atlantic from Icelandic ports.

In 1943, Admiral Ernest J. King, chief of U.S. naval forces, called representatives of the Allied nations together for the Atlantic Convoy Conference. Together they split the Atlantic into United States, British, and Canadian zones. This made each country responsible for protecting convoys within its own zone, allowing for continuous patrols over the entire ocean. The Allies adopted a system created by the British Royal Navy, nicknamed "Huff-Duff," to intercept radio signals sent from U-boats and establish the precise direction they came from. This information, in addition to the messages intercepted by the Allied code breakers, enabled Allied ships to pinpoint the exact location of every U-boat in the Atlantic and hunt them down within minutes. These developments gave the Allies the control of the ocean for the rest of the war. ✪

THE SINKING OF THE BISMARCK

The *Bismarck* was one of the Nazis' biggest ships—and in May 1941, the British navy made its destruction their primary mission. The *Bismarck* was on its way into the North Atlantic to disrupt British merchant ships. British intelligence spotted it off the coast of Norway, after receiving a tip from Swedish intelligence. The British navy sent two of its best ships, the battle cruiser *Hood* and the battleship *Prince of Wales*, after the *Bismarck*, and a vicious fight ensued. The *Hood* was destroyed and the *Prince of Wales* was seriously damaged. The *Bismarck* managed to hobble away. Thirty hours later, on May 26, a U.S. Navy pilot sighted the *Bismarck* 700 miles off the coast of France and a group of fighters torpedoed the *Bismarck* to prevent its escape. Within hours, British destroyers encircled the *Bismarck* and fighters dropped torpedoes throughout the night, which disabled the *Bismarck*'s steering and allowed for the battleships to attack the following morning. On May 27, the British battleships *King George V* and *Rodney* fired on the *Bismarck* for a solid hour, crippling the great ship. The conclusion to this battle is quite controversial. At 10:37 a.m., the cruiser *Dorsetshire* fired three torpedoes to finish off the legendary ship, but based upon research conducted upon the remains of the *Bismarck*, scientists and historians now support the conclusion that the battleship was sunk by its German commanders so that the Allies wouldn't be able to capture the ship or its crew.

May 24, 1941:
The German battleship *Bismarck*, the pride of the Nazi fleet, sinks the British cruiser *Hood*, killing 1,416 crewmen.

May 27, 1941:
The German battleship *Bismarck* is sunk by the British with most of its 2,200-man crew aboard.

Operation Barbarossa

Less than two years after its signing, the Nazi-Soviet Pact crumbled under the weight of panzer tanks and Adolf Hitler's desire to conquer all of Europe. On June 22, 1941, more than three million Axis troops swept into the Soviet Union in an invasion breathtaking in scale and devastation.

1. German invasion of Russia, Eastern Europe. 1941
2. Russian women digging tank traps during the siege of Leningrad.
3. A Russian mobile anti-tank unit moves up to the Stalingrad battlefront. October 1942
4. President Franklin D. Roosevelt signing Lend-Lease Extension.

The Germans began planning Operation Barbarossa in December 1940. Named after the Holy Roman Emperor Fredrick Barbarossa, the attack began on June 22, 1941 at 3:00 a.m. as more than 3,000 tanks and 2,500 aircraft swept eastward into the Soviet Union. Germany attacked in three thrusts along a front one thousand miles long. The invasion surprised Soviet Premier Stalin, who apparently expected continued neutrality with the Reich. Stalin had prepared inadequately but, nonetheless, Soviet forces were able to muster a large, though less technologically advanced, defense of nearly three million troops, more than 10,000 tanks, and 8,000 planes. Within two weeks, Axis forces had advanced hundreds of miles, and the Soviet Union had suffered nearly one million casualties.

Axis commanders sought to capture key Soviet cities in the northern, central, and southern regions of the nation. They pursued a scorched-earth policy, in which death squads followed the invading armies to massacre any remaining civilian, particularly Jewish populations. By the end of the year, Barbarossa had claimed 4.4 million Soviet casualties.

In the north, German forces laid siege to Leningrad (St. Petersburg), the Soviet Union's cultural and sometime political capital. It's difficult to know for certain how many people fell from disease, starvation, and wounds inflicted by German shells, but perhaps as many as one million residents died during the two-and-a-half-year siege.

In the center, panzer lines soon moved toward Moscow and were within twenty miles of the Soviet capital by the end of November 1941. On December 5, just as the tanks neared their ultimate goal, a surprise Soviet counterattack of 500,000 troops burst through a line of German forces weakened by worsening weather and a lack of reinforcements.

In the south, Axis forces swiftly captured the Ukrainian capital, Kiev, along with 600,000 Soviet troops. The invading armies included tens of thousands of troops from Germany, Hungary, Italy, and Romania, among other European nations. The battle in the southern region pivoted on the fate of Stalingrad (Volgograd), an industrial city named for the Soviet premier. Although Axis troops marched into the city on September 12, 1942, Stalin sent as many reinforcements as possible to hold the city at all costs. By the following February, Soviet forces had expelled the invaders at an enormous human toll. In total, the Battle

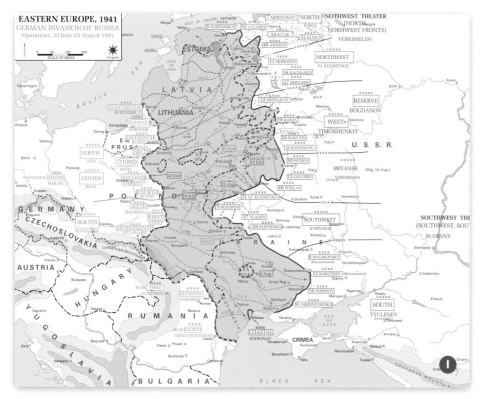

EASTERN EUROPE, 1941
GERMAN INVASION OF RUSSIA
Operations, 22 June–25 August 1941

June 22, 1941:
Operation Barbarossa begins when three million German troops march into the Soviet Union in a surprise attack.

Destroyed houses become strategic points for the Nazis in Stalingrad. During an attack they advance by running from house to house, wearing white wraps over their uniform as a winter camouflage. October 1942

July 12, 1941:
Britain and the Soviet Union sign a mutual aid treaty.

August 2, 1941:
Roosevelt extends the Lend-Lease Act to include the Soviet Union.

of Stalingrad resulted in combined casualties of two million, with 478,741 Soviets killed and an estimated 600,000 Axis troops killed in battle or as prisoners following the siege.

With forces bogged down in the north and south, and exhausted in Moscow, Nazi com- manders in Berlin received shocking details of losses unprecedented for Germany and the Axis powers. By January 1942, the Wehrmacht had suffered nearly one million casualties. The enor- mous losses from Barbarossa, which followed Germany's inability to defeat Britain, marked the beginning of the Nazi empire's retreat in Europe. Coupled with the entry of the United States into the war in December 1941, Germany faced increasingly dire odds as it entered 1942. Operation Barbarossa was and still is one of the biggest military invasions ever coordinated. ✪

ROOSEVELT'S LEND-LEASE PROGRAM

As the war in Europe raged on, British Prime Minister Winston Churchill asked President Roosevelt for assistance time and again. Though Roosevelt wanted to provide the Allies with weapons and equipment—especially because he felt that the longer the Allies could put up a strong fight, the longer the United States could keep its army out of the war—he was unable to do so without the authorization of Congress. In December 1940, President Roosevelt introduced a new program referred to as "Lend-Lease," which would enable the U.S. to send military vehicles, ammunition, or other material goods to any country important to the security of the U.S. Because the Allies could not afford to pay for the goods, the materials were either to be returned or paid for at some point after the end of the war. "Lend-Lease" also included the promise that the U.S. would gain access to military bases and other services owned by the Allies who received aid from America. In the meantime, the U.S. government would pay U.S. manufacturers for their products. Congress passed the Lend-Lease Act of 1941 in March, enabling the U.S. to provide immediate support to the Allies while officially remaining neutral. By the end of the war, the U.S. had provided between $48 and $50 billion in aid to more than thirty-eight countries with Great Britain, France, the Soviet Union, and China receiving the bulk of the aid.

August 18, 1941:
Hitler orders the last 76,000 Berlin Jews to be transferred to various ghettos in Poland.

September 1941:
The British agricultural ministry introduces Potato Pete, a character who encourages citizens to fill up on unrationed potatoes.

September 8, 1941:
The Nazis begin the siege of Leningrad (St. Petersburg) in the Soviet Union; it will last for nine hundred days (almost two and a half years).

The Day of Infamy

At 7:55 on the morning of Sunday, December 7, 1941, most sailors onboard the ships of the United States Pacific fleet at Pearl Harbor, Oahu, Hawaii, were enjoying a leisurely breakfast or perhaps were even still asleep when they heard the first explosions. A message broadcast from the commander on Ford Island to all ships in the area was "Air raid, Pearl Harbor. This is not [sic] drill!" The sailors sprang into action, but the odds were against them. The first and second wave of Japanese bombers, fighters, and torpedo planes—about 360 in all—had launched a surprise attack.

The ships were a perfect target, lined up side by side in Battleship Row. Within minutes, nearly every battleship had been hit by a bomb or torpedo. The *Arizona* was hit by an armor-piercing bomb that penetrated the deck and ignited more than one million pounds of gunpowder; the ship sank in less than nine minutes, killing 1,177 crew members. The *Oklahoma* was hit by torpedoes and capsized, trapping 429 men inside. The *California* and the *West Virginia* sank, the *Nevada* was beached, and the *Maryland* and *Pennsylvania* were all severely damaged, while the *Tennessee* suffered minor damage—and it was just the first wave of the attack.

Japanese planes attacked naval aircraft stationed at Ford Island and Kaneohe Bay Naval Air Stations and Marine aircraft at Ewa Marine Corps Air Station. They also surprised three U.S. Army Air Corps airfields—Bellows, Hickham, and Wheeler. At Hickham and Wheeler fighters dove within twenty-five feet of the ground and opened fire on U.S. planes resting wing to wing, parked close together to defend against sabotage. The setup was ideal for the enemy; the closely parked planes didn't have enough room to take off, and fires spread quickly from one plane to the next. A few planes were able to scramble into the air, but the United States was unable to mount an effective counterattack.

At approximately 8:45, a second wave of planes flew in and targeted the ships that hadn't already been hit. An hour later, the sky was quiet again. Twenty-one U.S. ships had been damaged or sunk (though all but three of them were

October 16, 1941:
Five hundred thousand women, children, and old men dig five thousand miles' worth of defensive trenches in and around Moscow.

October 17, 1941:
General Hideki Tojō becomes prime minister of Japan.

October 31, 1941:
America loses its first warship, the USS *Reuben James*, when it is torpedoed by a German U-boat as it escorts a group of ships carrying supplies to Britain.

> "Yesterday, December 7, 1941—a date which will live in infamy—the United States of America was suddenly and deliberately attacked by naval and air forces of the Empire of Japan."
>
> *—President Franklin D. Roosevelt, in a speech to Congress requesting that the United States officially declare war on Japan*

ultimately salvageable), 188 planes had been destroyed and an additional 159 had been damaged, 2,300 soldiers had been killed in the assault on Oahu; including civilians, the figure is 2,403, and 1,178 more people had been wounded. Within twenty-four hours, the Japanese also attacked the Pacific outposts of Malaya, Hong Kong, Guam, Wake Island, Midway Island, and the Philippines, attempting to take control of the Pacific before the United States could rally itself for a counterattack.

News of Pearl Harbor left the country in a state of shock. Everyone anxiously looked to the president for a response. At 12:30 p.m. the following day, President Roosevelt stood in front of Congress and delivered a speech that was simultaneously broadcast to the nation over the radio. More than 90 million American citizens, the largest radio audience in history, listened as the President asked Congress to declare war on Japan. Congress immediately voted in favor of the action, and the President signed the official declaration later that day. Britain followed suit, and within three days, the United States was at war with Germany and Italy as well. ✪

1. USS *Arizona* (BB-39) burns after the Japanese attack on Pearl Harbor. December 7, 1941
2. The front page of the Monday morning Extra edition of the *Los Angeles Times*, announces the Japanese air attack on Pearl Harbor, Hawaii. The newspaper reports that 350 people were killed in the attack. December 8, 1941
3. USS *Shaw* explodes during the Japanese raid on Pearl Harbor. December 7, 1941
4. Japanese General and Prime Minister Hideki Tojo. 1942
5. Damage at Pearl Harbor, Hawaii from Japanese attack. December 7, 1941

THE LEAD-UP TO WAR

The relationship between the United States and Japan had been spiraling downward for years. The U.S. was concerned by the aggressive behavior of Japan's military-led government since its full-scale invasion of China in 1937. In 1940, Japan aligned itself with the Axis Powers and declared its right to control all of Asia and the Pacific islands, including those that housed U.S. military bases. In an attempt to slow Japan down, the U.S. embargoed (restricted) shipments of petroleum and other vital war materials.

By the fall of 1941, the Japanese military leaders who were in control of the government were intent on war with the U.S. Though Japanese diplomats continued to negotiate with the U.S. up to the day of the Pearl Harbor attack, the government of Prime Minister Hideki Tojo put in motion the plans for war on November 25—the day six Japanese aircraft carriers set sail for Pearl Harbor. They thought that by destroying the U.S. fleet, they would force the U.S. to seek peace and allow Japan to continue with their plans in the Pacific. But they couldn't have been more wrong. After the attack, the U.S. was more intent on stopping Japan than ever before.

November 18, 1941:
British forces begin Operation Crusader on the North African front to stop Rommel's advances.

December 7, 1941:
The U.S. naval base at Pearl Harbor, Hawaii, is attacked by Japan. More than 2,300 American military men are killed.

December 8, 1941:
President Roosevelt signs a declaration of war against Japan.

President Franklin D. Roosevelt signing the declaration of war against Japan. December 8, 1941

1

2

The Home Front

3

Japan's attack at Pearl Harbor forged a national unity of purpose unparalleled in U.S. history. Within months of the assault, the American people had emerged from the economic hardships of the Great Depression to find themselves in a war. Unemployment plummeted and wages rose by 50 percent as military production soared. The emergence of defense industries brought in two million women workers, 10 percent of the female workforce.

1. War Bonds posters ca 1942–1943

2. Members of the community cultivate a field in preparation for a victory garden in support of the United States's efforts in the war. ca 1942

3. President Truman arrives on the Ellipse to pin the seventh Presidential Unit Citation on the 442nd Combat Infantry's colors. The unit was the most decorated combat unit of its size in U.S. history. Because of their bravery and that of African American soldiers in WWII, President Truman issued an order to desegregate the Armed Forces. July 15, 1946

4-5. Farmers and other evacuees of Japanese ancestry await an evacuation bus. They will be given opportunities to follow their callings at War Relocation Authority centers where they will spend the duration of the war. Centerville California. May 9, 1942

6. Following evacuation orders, this store, at 13th and Franklin Streets, has been closed. The owner, a University of California graduate of Japanese descent, has placed the "I AM AN AMERICAN" sign on the store-front on Dec. 8, the day after Pearl Harbor. Oakland, California.

7. Barrack homes at a War Relocation Authority center for evacuees of Japanese ancestry. Manzanar Relocation Center, Manzanar, California. April 5, 1942

In fundamental ways, the American home front differed greatly from other nations embroiled in the war. The contiguous forty-eight states did not experience the invading armies, bombing raids, and other horrors wrought upon the peoples of Europe, Africa, and Asia. Nonetheless, the nation of 131 million people experienced the emotional traumas of having 16.5 million of its citizens serve in the armed forces, with ten million drafted, 684,000 wounded, and 418,500 killed during their wartime service (including 292,131 killed in combat). Continuing a custom begun during World War I, millions of blue stars were hung outside homes of military members. These public symbols of service were covered in silver if the person was wounded and gold in case of death.

In addition to the emotional and physical scars of combat, the American home front tensed with the possibility of an enemy attack. Ten million people joined the Office of Civilian Defense, which aided local defense preparations and facilitated citizen support of the war effort. Teenagers volunteered as air-raid marshals, and children joined scrap drives to collect metal, rubber, paper, cooking grease (for bomb making), and other items needed by the military.

The federal government imposed strict rationing of household items, including coffee, sugar, meat, tires, canned goods, and even shoes. Beginning in 1942, adults and children received ration books, with individual coupons to be exchanged for groceries. Later in the conflict, the government instituted a points system, whereby each person was allotted a certain number of points per month to be exchanged for meat and

December 10, 1941:
Japan invades the Philippines.

December 11, 1941:
Germany and Italy declare war on the United States; the United States declares war on them.

January 1, 1942:
Because of the need to conserve steel for the war effort, the sale of new cars and trucks is suspended in the United States.

processed foods. The speed limit dropped to thirty-five miles per hour nationwide, and drivers received automobile stickers to mark their gasoline rations.

Yet the American people joined together to accept these restrictions with few complaints, perceiving these regulations as essential steps to winning the war. For instance, in 1943, families and communities across the country created 20.5 million "Victory Gardens," which provided fruits and vegetables to reduce demand for rationed food. Added together, these gardens covered land the size of Rhode Island and provided one-third of all of the vegetables eaten in the United States that year.

Faced with the challenge of quickly raising money to mount the war effort, the federal government began selling Victory Bonds in May 1941. Eighty-five million Americans, two-thirds of the population, soon purchased bonds worth $157 billion.

Fictional characters from Bugs Bunny to Captain America encouraged young adults to do whatever they could to aid the cause. Cultural icons not only encouraged others to sacrifice for national defense but real-life stars such as Boston Red Sox slugger Ted Williams and heavyweight boxing champion Joe Louis enlisted in the military as well. In fact, hundreds of pro football and baseball players served during the war, as their respective leagues continued to play games as necessary entertainment for a unified, dedicated public. These innumerable selfless acts at home played no small part in winning the war—and prepared the nation for the domestic and global challenges of the postwar era. ✪

JAPANESE INTERNMENT

On February 19, 1942, President Roosevelt signed Executive Order 9066, which enabled the designation of military areas from which people may be excluded for "protection against espionage and against sabotage." In the wake of Japan's assault on Pearl Harbor, civilians and military officers alike understood that this vague declaration endorsed the removal of people of Japanese descent from the Pacific Coast. Although no one of Japanese descent living in the United States was ever

United States. The ten internment camps were located in California, the Rocky Mountain states, and as far east as Arkansas. The smallest camp held 7,318 people in Granada, Colorado, and the largest contained 18,789 in Tule Lake, California. The first camp opened on May 5, 1942, and the last one closed on March 20, 1946, though most internees had been released prior to the end of the war. In 1988, the federal government passed legislation that provided $20,000 in reparation to each surviving internee. Histori-

charged with espionage or sabotage during the war, desire for revenge, fear of a Japanese invasion, and a desire to confiscate valuable Japanese-American-owned property spurred the internment program.

Within several months, more than 110,000 people of Japanese descent were forcibly relocated from the West Coast. These internees included 70,000 American citizens, imprisoned for their ancestral links to a nation at war with the

ans estimate that the internees lost more than half a billion dollars in property because of their imprisonment.

Despite the internment camps and waves of anti-Japanese propaganda, thousands of Japanese-Americans volunteered for duty in the U.S. armed services. The highly decorated 442nd Regimental Combat Team, comprised of 3,500 Japanese-Americans, many of whom came from interned families, served with distinction and valor in North Africa and Italy.

January 13, 1942:
Operation Drumroll begins, where Germany moves U-boats to the waters off the American East Coast to disrupt American shipping lanes.

January 20, 1942:
The Nazis plan the "Final Solution," the genocide of Europe's Jewish population, at the Wannsee Conference in Berlin.

January 26, 1942:
The first U.S. troops arrive in Britain.

Spies, Code Breakers, and Saboteurs

Secrecy was of the utmost importance to diplomatic and military strategy during the war. Axis and Allied nations employed a diverse collection of strategies to deceive, outwit, and catch their opponent by surprise. Just as important as undertaking secret operations was preserving the secrecy of one's own plans. From Normandy to Midway, secrecy proved of the utmost importance and often held the key to victory in battle.

Whether the subjects concerned diplomatic affairs or military strategy, coded messages required complex encrypting to ensure that messages could not be read by the enemy. The German Enigma cipher (encoding) machine, one of the most famous code makers of the war, featured a typewriter keyboard attached to a series of rotating discs. With each key press, the discs rotated, punching a different letter each time. Only someone with the exact specifications for the system of rotations would be able to decrypt the messages typed into Enigma.

The actual work of cracking, or decrypting, enemy code was lonely and tedious, but success, as impressed officers commented, rivaled pure magic. Code breakers benefited from the simple fact that, despite millions of possible letter combinations in a code, there are only a certain number of letters in the alphabet. By 1940, the French, British, and Polish had cracked Enigma, and Allied commanders relied upon German messages to monitor troop movements, battle plans, and diplomatic strategies during the war. In June 1943, Britain and the United States agreed to share their intelligence concerning the Axis, with Britain responsible for German communications and the United States for Japanese messages.

Perhaps more than in Europe, decryption proved pivotal in the Pacific war. U.S. code breakers successfully cracked both the Japanese military (JN-25) and diplomatic ("Purple") codes. Throughout the war, U.S. intelligence knew of Japanese tactics and often could relay that information to commanders in the field prior to battle. At the Battle of Midway, U.S. naval officers learned of the Japanese navy's route, revised their strategy, and ambushed the larger forces. The victory at Midway in 1942 provided the United States with a massive boost of morale and brought devastating losses to the Japanese fleet.

February 13, 1942:
Hitler cancels Operation Sea Lion, the planned German invasion of Britain.

February 19, 1942:
Japanese forces attack the islands of Bali, Mandalay, and Timor.

February 27–March 1, 1942:
The Allies are defeated by the Japanese in the Battle of the Java Sea, which allows the Japanese to freely move about the Indonesian waters.

March 17, 1942:
General Douglas MacArthur lands in Darwin, Australia, taking on his role as leader of the Allied troops in the Southwest Pacific Theater.

NAVAJO CODE TALKERS

O f the 25,000 American Indians who served in the U.S. armed forces during World War II, 400 Navajo, "code talkers" played an integral role in military operations in Europe and the Pacific. Desperate to devise a method of encryption that could not be broken by the Axis, the code talkers constructed a code based upon the Navajo language that proved impossible for enemy forces to break. At the time, only a handful of non-Navajo people understood the language, making Navajo perfect for code making. The code used Navajo words associated with nature to correspond to certain military terms—turtle for tank, for instance. Serving in the U.S. Marine Corps, the code talkers participated in every single Marine operation in the Pacific war. They transmitted and decoded hundreds of messages rapidly and effectively during military operations, including battles at Okinawa and Iwo Jima. In addition to the Navajo in the Pacific, Comanche, Choctaw, Chippewa, and code talkers from other Native American nations also served in Europe, including at D-Day.

5

The Signal Intelligence Service (SIS) and the Office of Naval Intelligence led U.S. code breaking efforts and always needed to keep their projects absolutely secret. If the enemy learned that their code had been decrypted, then they would work to craft a new one or create fake messages to distract their opponent.

In spy actions, the same rule held true, as compromised operatives could threaten a mission's success and a spy's safety. American singer Josephine Baker spied on Nazis and avoided detection by sending messages written in invisible ink to officers with French intelligence. During the war, the Office of Strategic Services (OSS) led U.S. spy operations, later becoming the Central Intelligence Agency (CIA). But the OSS was not the only office to run clandestine programs during the war. The Military Intelligence Service's Escape and Evasion Section was devoted to helping 95,532 American POWs held in Europe. With the aid of this office, 737 of these POWs escaped. The Escape and Evasion Section utilized devices ranging from baseballs with radios hidden inside to cameras packaged within matchboxes to help prisoners secretly communicate with their allies.

In addition to espionage, saboteurs also proved critical to the Allied effort. Forms of sabotage ranged from well-structured assaults on enemy bases to individual attempts to weaken the opposition. The French resistance attacked German transportation and communication lines to coincide with the D-Day attack. They cut telephone lines, blocked railroad cars, and set fire to ships to hamper the flow of German reinforcements to northern France.

Given the importance of secrecy in creating missions, Axis and Allied commanders often utilized deception to gain the upper hand. The most famous example of this came with Operation Fortitude prior to the D-Day invasion. Allied forces devised an entirely fictional army group, including fake equipment, soldiers, planes, buildings, and ships. The critical component of the ruse, though, lay with the sending of a series of coded messages that Allied intelligence knew German code breakers could decipher. The messages disclosed details for a massive assault to occur after June 6, 1944 (D-Day) and farther north up the Normandy coastline. The trick worked so well that Hitler never sent sufficient reinforcements following the beginning of Operation Overlord, and even after the Normandy invasion had begun in earnest, he continued to hold back supplementary forces, believing that a larger attack at a different location was about to occur. ☸

1. American-born entertainer, dancer, and singer Josephine Baker (right) as a volunteer in the Free French Women's Air Auxiliary. ca 1940
2. Computer pioneer Alan Turing, who helped crack German Enigma codes during WWII. United Kingdom. 1951
3. Wreckage from a Nazi fuel supply train that was blown up and derailed by the French Patriots near Waremine-Le-Grand in France. It held up rail traffic for five days. November 28, 1943
4. A German cipher machine, code-named Enigma, which was developed by H. A. Koch in 1919 and used by German intelligence up until World War II. The ULTRA code system was cracked by a polish group of cryptoanalysts in the 1930s.
5. Navajo Indian Code Talkers Henry Bake and George Kirk. December 12, 1943

March 18, 1942:
Lord Louis Mountbatten is appointed to the post as Chief of Combined Operations by the Americans and British.

April 10, 1942:
The Bataan Death March begins when 70,000 to 80,000 American and Filipino troops surrender to the Japanese in the Bataan Peninsula.

Japanese troops guard American and Filipino prisoners in Bataan, Philippines after their capture of the Bataan Peninsula on April 9, 1942. The prisoners were later forced to march over 100 kilometres from Bataan to Tarlac in what became known as the Bataan Death March.

Women in the War

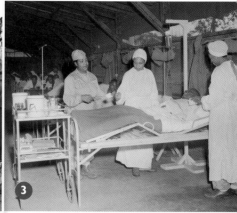

I n a war governed exclusively by men, women devoted their work, their families, and their lives to the conflict. In Allied and Axis nations alike, women played an integral role in the war effort, working in wartime industries, in farming, in public aid positions, and, in some instances, in military service.

In December 1941, Great Britain instituted a labor draft of women to fill the jobs left by men who had become soldiers. During the war, women became a majority of the workforce in the Soviet Union and began fighting in combat in 1942. These female soldiers served as pilots, tank drivers, and snipers. In the United States, more than 350,000 women served in the military. They worked in the women's units attached to the military branches, including the Women's Army Corps (WAC), the Army Nurse Corps, Women Auxiliary Service Pilots (WASPS/Army Air Corps), Women Accepted for Volunteer Emergency Service (WAVES/Navy), and Semper Paratus, meaning "always ready" (SPARS/Coast Guard).

On the American home front, the Office of War Information and the War Manpower Commission created Rosie the Riveter and other advertisements encouraging women to work in war-related industries. On posters headlined "We Can Do It!," Rosie appeared confident, strong, and determined to roll up her sleeves and aid the war effort. Inspired by the opportunity to work for national defense and for a decent wage, two million women gained war-related industrial employ-

ment. Overall, the number of women in the U.S. workforce rose by 50 percent, or six million people, during the war.

While many American women eagerly joined the labor force, they still retained their prewar responsibilities as primary caregivers at home. About 25 percent of adult American women worked outside of the home during the war, a higher percentage than in Germany or Japan but far below rates in Britain and the Soviet Union. In addition to maintaining family households, women devoted themselves to maintaining a home front in which sixteen million men, more than 10 percent of the national population, had been thrust into military service. Women directed domestic conservation efforts, grew Victory Gardens, ran civil defense programs, led war-bond drives, rationed groceries, reused and recycled countless household items, educated the young, and cared for children, the elderly, and the hundreds of thousands of wounded soldiers who returned from combat.

In the United States and throughout the world, women's wartime service at home and abroad underscored their power and self-reliance. For many women, it was the first time that they worked outside their homes and earned a paycheck. The public victories for women during the war established a new set of social, political, and economic expectations that inspired millions of women to struggle for equal rights in the coming decades. ✪

April 18, 1942:
U.S. B-25 bombers launched from the USS *Hornet* carry out a surprise first attack on Tokyo, a raid the Japanese had thought impossible.

May 4–8, 1942:
In the Battle of the Coral Sea, the Allies foil a Japanese attack on Port Moresby in New Guinea. This is the first major setback for the Japanese in the war.

May 14, 1942:
Congress creates the U.S. Women's Army Auxiliary Corps (WAAC), allowing for uniformed service of women. The next day, President Roosevelt signs it into law.

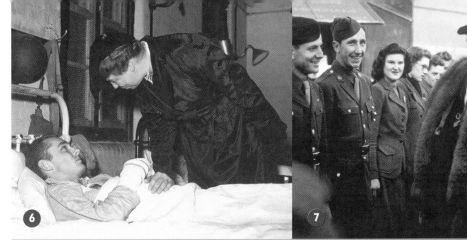

1. United States Army Nurse flies with the wounded. 1942–1945
2. Maj. Charity E. Adams and Capt. Abbie N. Campbell inspect the first contingent of Negro members of the Women's Army Corps assigned to overseas service. England. February 15, 1945
3. Surgical ward treatment at the 268th Station Hospital, Base A, Milne Bay, New Guinea. Left to right: Sgt. Lawrence McKreever, patient; 2nd Lt. Prudence Burns, ward nurse; 2nd Lt. Elcena Townscent, chief surgical nurse; and an unidentified nurse. June 22, 1944
4. War poster: Rosie the Riveter. ca. 1942–1943
5. War poster. 1941–1945
6. Eleanor Roosevelt (right), wife of American President Franklin Delano Roosevelt, visits a wounded U.S. soldier recovering in a hospital. United Kingdom. 1942
7. Eleanor Roosevelt talks to U.S. soldiers during a visit to a Fighter Factory in Birmingham.
8. Women's Army Corps members in battle gear with packs walk up gangplank to board ship bound for France.

ELEANOR ROOSEVELT

As the public "eyes and ears" of the longest-serving president in U.S. history, Eleanor Roosevelt recast the position of First Lady and imbued it with unprecedented purpose and vigor. A distant cousin of Franklin Delano Roosevelt, Eleanor overcame her shyness to become a force in American politics and culture that well suited the energy of FDR's administration. Arguably the most controversial, powerful, and inspiring First Lady, she spoke out on controversial issues and, in particular, strove to improve the status of women and African-Americans. During World War II, Eleanor campaigned for integration of the armed forces, protection for refugees, and employment of women in war-related industries. She wrote a regular newspaper column, "My Day," and served briefly as the assistant director of the Office of Civilian Defense, providing inspiration for millions of women to join the war effort. After FDR's death, Eleanor remained in public life, continuing her struggles for civil rights and equality until her death in 1962.

"We Can Do It!"

—Artist J. Howard Miller, produced for the Westinghouse War Production Coordinating Committee, 1942

May 27, 1942:
The British deploy the high-tech American-made Grant M3 tank against Rommel's troops in Libya.

June 4–6, 1942:
The Allies achieve a remarkable victory in the Battle of Midway, sinking four of Japan's six largest aircraft carriers.

June 18, 1942:
Bernard Robinson, a Harvard medical student, becomes the first African-American ensign in the U.S. Naval Reserve.

The War in the Pacific

Coming on the heels of the "three alls" campaign in China—"Kill all, burn all, destroy all"—Japanese officials attacked Allied forces in Hawaii, the Philippines, Singapore, Burma, Hong Kong, and the Dutch East Indies (Indonesia) in December 1941. This terrifying path of conquest caused swift defeats for the Allies and devastation for local populations. Japan quickly defeated British forces in Burma and American forces stationed in the Philippines, which had been an American protectorate since the Spanish-American War.

In the Bataan Peninsula, on the Philippine island of Luzon, Japanese forces captured 80,000 Allied troops after a lengthy siege. These prisoners of war then began what came to be known as the Bataan Death March. This march stretched sixty-five miles through thick jungle and endured for nearly three years. The captured soldiers experienced gruesome treatment along the way, including torture, mutilation, and murder. By the time they reached their destination, 600 American and 10,000 Filipino prisoners had died. Thousands more perished in the months after the POWs reached camp.

Few expected any assault on Japan's main islands in the months following Pearl Harbor. The distances seemed too far for reconstructing American forces to target successfully. Yet, on April 18, 1942,

CRACKING JAPANESE CODE

Two years prior to Pearl Harbor, U.S. intelligence faced the daunting task of breaking the Japanese diplomatic code, code-named "Purple." The Purple encryption machine looked like a pair of keyboards attached by a maze of wires and switches. When the code maker typed a message into one keyboard, the machine altered the text through a series of steps that encrypted the message further and further, so that the text ultimately typed by the second attached typewriter appeared completely different from the original message. No American had ever seen the Purple encryption machine (and no Purple machine survived the war). Nonetheless, a determined group of code breakers pursued the machine's formula by trial and error, guesswork, and, most important, by tracking consistencies from message to message. By noting that certain terms were repeated, such as for dates or locations, code breakers could build upon these findings to unlock more and more code segments. By September 1940, they had cracked Purple, and their work was code-named "Magic" out of respect for this code breaking feat. After they'd broken the code, the cryptanalysts created their own Purple machines so that they could decrypt messages in a matter of days and sometimes hours. "Magic" enabled U.S. intelligence to read communication between Japanese government officials and diplomats serving around the world.

July 6, 1942:
Jewish teenager Anne Frank and her family go into hiding as the Nazis round up the Jewish population in Amsterdam. Anne records her experiences in a diary.

July 26, 1942:
Britain begins rationing sweets and chocolate, limiting purchases to a half pound per person every four weeks.

July 30, 1942:
The U.S. Navy establishes a military reserve for women, called Women Appointed for Voluntary Emergency Service (WAVES).

"I'm in this war too!" Women's Army Corps. 1941–1945

"I'm in this war too!"

WOMEN'S ARMY CORPS
ARMY OF THE UNITED STATES

"I shall return."

—General MacArthur, as he leaves the Philippines for a new command post in Australia in 1942

Lieutenant Colonel James Doolittle led a squadron of 16 B-25 bombers on an 800-mile bombing raid over Tokyo and a few other Japanese cities. Running out of fuel on their overextended missions, the group crash-landed in China, with several of the pilots soon captured by Japanese forces. The Doolittle Raid waged a heavy psychological toll on the Japanese home front. The attack revealed critical weaknesses in Japan's defense capabilities and spurred Allied efforts to target the Japanese mainland as soon as possible.

In the Battle of the Coral Sea in early May 1942, the U.S. and Japanese navies pounded each other in an engagement famous for their ships never closing within sight of each other. The battle ushered in a new era where aircraft carriers dominated naval warfare. Both fleets launched wave after wave of fighter squadrons, in attempts to strike their enemy's fleets from the air. U.S. forces succeeded in preventing Japan from moving farther south toward Australia.

The stalemate in the Coral Sea set the stage for the Battle of Midway one month later. From June 4 to 7, 1942, the U.S. Navy engaged the Japanese fleet near Midway, an island of critical importance to both American and Japanese naval forces. Having cracked Japan's military code (JN-25), U.S. Admiral Nimitz knew of Japanese Admiral Yamamoto's strategy in advance and positioned his warships to take the Japanese fleet by surprise. During the battle, U.S. forces destroyed four of the six aircraft carriers that partici-

pated in the attack on Pearl Harbor. The defeat reversed the balance of power in the Pacific.

Following the victory at Midway, the U.S. Navy again moved to block Japanese advances in the Solomon Islands toward Australia. The Battle of Guadalcanal Island began the so-called island campaigns of the Pacific war, with outnumbered Japanese soldiers fighting from entrenched positions on confined island battlefields. Beginning on August 7, 1942, the Battle of Guadalcanal lasted into February 1943, with more than 50,000 Marines fighting 30,000 Japanese troops on the small island, in addition to constant naval bombardments of the island from the sea. In prolonged combat in dense, malaria-infested forests, more than two-thirds of the Japanese troops on the island died, including nearly 10,000 from starvation and disease. The United States suffered 6,111 casualties, including 1,752 killed on the island, but succeeded due to greater reinforcements of men and machines than Japan. This pattern of battle would repeat itself over and over again in the coming months.

Mirroring the successes and failures of Nazi Germany in Europe, Japan's initial victories brought waves of terror, death, and destruction to millions of people across thousands of miles of land and sea. Yet these advances planted the seeds for Japan's ultimate downfall, as its military became overcommitted, overextended, and unable to marshal the resources necessary to continue such a massive campaign. ✪

1. U.S. Navy Grumman Hellcats line astern in readiness for take off against the Japanese forces in Manila. Plane handlers pass signals to pilots as the take offs get underway. ca 1945

2. The largest of three surviving pieces of the famous Japanese diplomatic cipher machine, it was recovered from the wreckage of the Japanese Embassy in Berlin. 1945

3. Japanese bomber pilots receive their orders on board an aircraft carrier prior to commencing their mission of bombing Pearl Harbor. December 7, 1941

4. U.S. Admiral Chester Nimitz during the fight to retake the Marshall Islands. February 1944

5. Japanese soldiers march prisoners of war, with arms raised, across the Bataan Peninsula in what became known as the Batan Death March. Luzon, Philippines. mid-April 1942.

August 7, 1942:
American Marines invade the Solomon Islands of Guadalcanal and Tulagi.

General Douglas MacArthur wades ashore during initial landings at Leyte, Philippine Islands. October 1944

August 26, 1942:
An Axis force of 500,000 German and Romanian soldiers attack the Soviets just outside of Stalingrad.

October 23, 1942:
The American M4 Sherman tank is employed for the first time at the Second Battle of El Alamein in Egypt.

Operation Torch

esitant to engage German forces on the European continent, Allied commanders perceived North Africa as the most likely avenue of success against the Axis in the region. The Allies hoped that victory there would provide a foothold on the Mediterranean Sea from which to launch an invasion northward into Italy.

In the first battle at El Alamein, Egypt, in July 1942, Allied forces finally succeeded in stalling Rommel's advance from Libya into Egypt. From October 23 to November 5, 1942, Allied divisions under the command of Bernard Montgomery again defeated Rommel in pivotal combat that turned the tide of the North African campaign. Montgomery marshaled more than double the men (220,000) and tanks (1,100) to block Axis expansion in Africa and pave the way for a larger invasion of Allied forces.

On November 8, 1942, U.S. General Dwight D. Eisenhower launched Operation Torch, an amphibious assault that rivaled the later D-Day invasion in its investment of soldiers, ships, and artillery. The success of the landings in Morocco and Algeria enabled the Allies to control over 1,300 miles of North African coastline within just three days. More than 65,000 Allied troops participated in the assault, with the goal of moving eastward to connect with Montgomery's forces and ultimately surrounding Rommel's panzer forces.

Victories in November and December 1942 perhaps left Allied commanders overconfident. On January 19, 1943, Rommel mobilized his panzer forces at the Kasserine Pass, a two-mile-long passageway between mile-high mountains in Tunisia. In a surprise assault on grossly outnumbered Allied tank divisions, the larger Axis force swept through enemy lines and caused a reappraisal of Allied strategy in North Africa.

Eisenhower used this time as an opportunity to regroup, building his troop and tank levels to match Rommel's group. Eisenhower also installed well-known tank strategist General George S. Patton to lead the reinforced army into battle. Though controversial in his methods, Patton

NORTH AFRICA, 1941
THE ALLIED INVASION, 8 NOVEMBER 1942

0   50   100   150   200
SCALE OF MILES

SPAIN

MEDITERRAN

EASTERN TASK FORCE

CENTER TASK FORCE

Boug

Gibraltar

Algiers

WESTERN TASK FORCE

Tangier

Oran

La Senia
Tafaraoui

SPANISH MOROCCO

Oujda

ATLANTIC OCEAN

Sale
Rabat   Port
Lyautey   Fez
Casablanca   Meknes
Fedala
Mazagan

A L G E R

M O R O C C O

Safi

Mogador   Marrakech

2

"Nothing but latrine rumors. All the Americans can

November 8, 1942:
Allied forces launch Operation Torch in North Africa, invading Casablanca in Morocco and Oran and Algiers in Algeria.

November 22, 1942:
The Soviet's Red Army surrounds 270,000 German troops, trapping them in Stalingrad with few supplies just as the harsh Russian winter arrives.

December 1, 1942:
The United States begins rationing gas to its citizens.

30

BERNARD MONTGOMERY

The most famous British military officer of the war, Field Marshal Bernard Montgomery led Allied victories in several key battles in North Africa and Europe. Like so many of his fellow commanders, Montgomery entered the Second World War as a combat veteran of World War I. His experience led him to be a deliberate, overly cautious, well-organized field director. In October 1942, his army's win at the second El Alamein battle spurred the Allies' eventual victory in North Africa and earned his promotion to general. He later led Allied forces in the Sicilian and Normandy invasions, as well as during the Battle of the Bulge and the subsequent advance into Germany. His skills as a planner and tactician greatly aided Allied preparations for D-Day, and his service during Operation Overlord earned his promotion to field marshal on September 1, 1944. Faced with the ongoing challenge of leading both U.S. and British forces, Montgomery became an increasingly controversial figure—popular with his troops but criticized by American commanders for his seemingly limitless patience in the face of various crises and their calls for immediate action. On May 4, 1945, Montgomery accepted the surrender of German forces in northern Europe, spanning northwest Germany, Denmark, and the Netherlands.

1. American General Dwight D. Eisenhower watches tank exercise during tour of Allied forces before the invasion of Normandy. 1944
2. The Allied Invasion, North Africa. 1941
3. Dwight D. Eisenhower (center), British Field Marshal Bernard L. Montgomery (right), and Air Marshal Sir Arthur Tedder (left) during a Supreme Command Tour. 1944
4. American soldiers aboard small landing craft during the opening hours of Operation Torch, the Allied invasion of Vichy French controlled western North Africa.
5. Adolf Hitler (center) and Marshal of the Reich, Hermann Goering (right) receive a briefing outdoors from a uniformed Nazi officer of the Richthofen Squadron. ca 1943

achieved great success in reforming the command structure and improving troop morale. His forces restarted the drive east to join Montgomery's forces, sandwiching the Axis forces in Tunisia. On May 12, 1943, the Allied plan came to fruition as the combined forces of Montgomery and Patton broke the Axis lines and captured more than 200,000 prisoners. The Allied victory in North Africa provided a base of operations for the long-anticipated invasion of the European mainland, beginning in Sicily and then the Italian mainland in summer 1943. ✪

make are razor blades and refrigerators."

—Hermann Goering, in response to a report of British troops destroying his tanks with American-made ammunition

December 2, 1942:
Physicists Enrico Fermi and Arthur Compton create the first controlled nuclear chain reaction, a major step toward making an atomic bomb.

Dr. Enrico Fermi and Dr. Arthur Compton

January 18, 1943:
Having learned of the mass murders occurring at the concentration camps, Jews in the Warsaw ghetto stage an uprising against their Nazi captors with improvised weapons and explosives.

January 31, 1943:
German Field Marshal Friedrich Paulus surrenders to the Red Army at Stalingrad, but the remainder of his army do not turn themselves in until three days later.

Weapons of War

From tanks to rockets to battleships to even balloons, many of the weapons utilized during World War II originated years before the conflict. Yet the war saw unprecedented experimentation, invention, and development of the implements of war. Technological advances enabled the design of stronger, faster, and more powerful vehicles.

Aircraft carriers, amphibious tanks, and other machines removed the boundaries between zones of engagement. Military commanders used carriers to launch air forces for attacks against the enemy in the air, on land, or at sea.

Carrier strength proved critical to the Pacific war, with carriers serving as mobile bases, able to launch strikes hundreds, or even thousands, of miles from their targets. Amphibious tanks and transport vehicles allowed for the movement of massive forces to invade enemy lines on land and

by sea. Used in all theaters of the war, amphibious technology played a critical role in Operation Torch (the invasion of North Africa) and Operation Overlord (the invasion of France).

Bombs and artillery had existed for centuries, but advancements in design made their use far more devastating during World War II. Incendiary bombs, nearly 100,000 tons of which were dropped by U.S. bombers on Japan, created raging firestorms upon impact. Defensive units placed hundreds of millions of mines on land and

in the sea, manufactured to explode if touched by enemy forces. Germany developed guns stationed on railroad lines, capable of shooting artillery nearly thirty miles. The United States M1 howitzer had a range of two miles, capable of targeting ships docked off the coast or distant panzer lines.

Military technicians used more than iron and steel to forge their weaponry. American gun makers harvested silk from black widow spiders to make aiming crosshairs for sniper rifles. The

1. USS *Essex* based TBMs and SB2Cs drop bombs on Hokadate (sic: Hakodate), Japan
2. Front view of 240mm howitzer of Battery. "B", 697th Field Artillery Battalion, just before firing into German-held territory. Mignano area, Italy. January 30, 1944
3. The "Little Boy" atom bomb which was dropped on Hiroshima, Japan, by the United States on August 6, 1945.
4. 16 inch guns of the USS *Iowa* fire during battle drill in the Pacific. ca. 1944
5. Manhattan Project head J. Robert Oppenheimer, atomic physicist leading team in developing atomic bomb. 1954
6. A dense column of smoke rises more than 60,000 feet into the air over the Japanese port of Nagasaki, the result of an atomic bomb, the second ever used in warfare, dropped on the industrial center on August 8, 1945, from a U.S. B-29 Superfortress.

February 4, 1943:
The Combined Chiefs of Staff assign General Eisenhower command of all the Allied forces in North Africa.

May 12, 1943:
The battle for North Africa is over when all Axis forces there officially surrender.

June 11, 1943:
SS chief Heinrich Himmler orders the remaining Jews in Poland be relocated to concentration camps.

> # "Now I am become Death, the destroyer of worlds."
> *—J. Robert Oppenheimer, July 16, 1945*

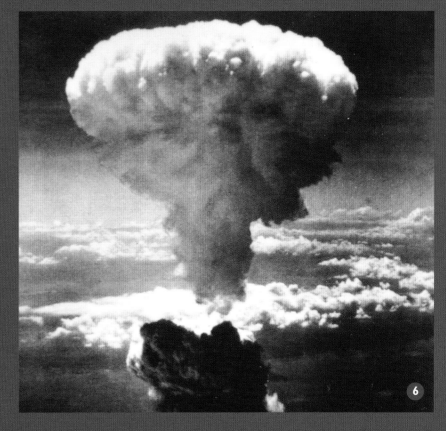

controversial Japanese military Unit 731 developed biological weapons for use against enemy troops and civilian populations. Unit 731 created bombs containing fleas infected with plague. The unit also released typhus and other diseases into water supplies and tested other biological weapons on civilian prisoners.

Japan also utilized a centuries-old technology—the balloon—to strike the continental United States. More than 9,000 balloon bombs were sent from Japan, catching the jet stream and floating 5,000 miles across the Pacific Ocean. Possessing no guidance system and only rudimentary altitude controls, nearly 300 are confirmed to have reached North America. In fact, the only American civilians killed in the continental United States during the war were victims of one of these devices. On March 5, 1945, six people died when they accidentally detonated a balloon bomb they found while picnicking in Oregon.

On the other end of the spectrum, the most prominent technological advancement in weaponry during the war was the atomic bomb. The U.S. Manhattan Project encompassed an unprecedented degree of technological, scientific, and economic investment. With the atomic bombings of Japan, World War II concluded with the invention of weapons technology that made many wartime military innovations almost instantly obsolete. ✪

MANHATTAN PROJECT

With so many advances in weaponry during the war, the Allied and Axis powers raced to devise a new weapon that promised victory to any who possessed it— the atomic bomb. Scientists in the United States, the Soviet Union, Great Britain, Japan, and Germany worked countless hours in search of the right formula for constructing a nuclear weapon, one that would unleash the power of splitting the atom. Secretary of War Henry Stimson predicted the bomb to be "the most terrifying weapon ever known in human history." Unmatched in its investment in atomic research and development, the U.S. Army Corps of Engineers directed the Manhattan Project to create a usable atomic bomb as quickly as possible. The project, kept under the utmost secrecy until after the war, cost an estimated $2 billion and employed 150,000 people. J. Robert Oppenheimer led the scientific team, comprised of some of the nation's foremost minds, as well as German scientists who had escaped from Nazi Germany. On July 16, 1945, the Manhattan Project's work came to fruition with the detonation of a sphere of plutonium the size of a grapefruit. The so-called Trinity Test at Alamogordo, New Mexico, produced an explosion that equaled 12,500 tons of TNT and created temperatures thousands of times hotter than the sun. Upon reflection of witnessing the Trinity Test, Oppenheimer quoted an ancient Hindu text: "Now I am become death, the destroyer of worlds." Within a month, U.S. forces had dropped two atomic bombs on the Japanese cities of Hiroshima and Nagasaki, ending the war and ushering in a new era of human history.

June 21, 1943:
SS chief Heinrich Himmler orders that all remaining Jews in the occupied Soviet Union be relocated to concentration camps.

Jews wait on a Warsaw street for deportation to a concentration camp. Poland, ca 1944.

July 10, 1943:
More than 150,000 Allied soldiers invade Sicily in Operation Husky.

July 12, 1943:
The Germans continue their offensive on the Eastern Front at Kursk with the largest tank battle recorded.

The Allies Invaded Italy

After victory in North Africa in May 1943, U.S. and British strategists set their sights on Italy as the weakest point to begin their invasion of Europe. The Italian assault would enable continued preparations for a larger invasion to take place in northern France in 1944.

1. Fliers of a P-51 Mustang Group of the 15th Air Force in the shadow of one of their Mustangs., Italy. ca. August 1944
2. American troops wade ashore from a landing craft during the invasion of Salerno, Italy.
3. General George S. Pattoon
4. Allied invasion of Italy with planned German delaying positions, Italy 1944
5. The "Big Three" (left to right) Joseph Stalin, American President Franklin Roosevelt, and British Prime Minister Winston Churchill. November/ December 1943

The two iconic field leaders of the Allied armies—Britain's General Bernard Montgomery and U.S. General George S. Patton—joined their forces to launch a massive assault on the island of Sicily, at the southern tip of the "boot" of Italy. Before daybreak on July 10, 1943, 180,000 Allied troops and more than 2,500 ships participated in the largest amphibious operation until the D-Day invasion one year later. Allied forces encountered larger Axis defenses of 350,000 Italians and Germans.

On July 22, the Allies captured the Sicilian port of Palermo, and Italian King Victor Emmanuel III removed Benito Mussolini from power three days later. More than 100,000 Italian troops were taken prisoner as support for the war waned, and, by August 17, the Axis had surrendered Sicily. With Mussolini removed from power, the new Italian leadership signed an armistice, or cease-fire agreement, with the Allies on September 3, 1943. Fearful of attacks by Italians still fighting with the Axis and Wehrmacht troops stationed throughout the country, the armistice was not announced until five days later.

On September 9, 1943, days after smaller Allied landings began in southern Italy, Operation Avalanche began. Using Sicily and North Africa as launching points for the full-scale invasion of Italy, Allied forces landed at the city of Salerno and began the slow, difficult advance northward to Rome. Established south of Rome, the so-called Gustav Line included 130,000 Wehrmacht troops who were dug in and well fortified. Though the Allies reached Naples on October 1, they could not penetrate the Gustav Line. Searching for an alternate route to Rome, Allied commanders launched a series of landings at Anzio, only fifty miles from Rome and behind the Wehrmacht line, on January 22, 1944. But progress was slow and costly, with German forces able to hold their ground for months.

The battle for Italy endangered thousands of historical artifacts, priceless works of art, and centuries-old buildings. In February 1944, Allied bombers struck a monastery at Monte Cassino that dated to the sixth

July 25, 1943:
Rebellious generals and opposing politicians overthrow and arrest Mussolini and disband the fascist political party in Italy.

September 3, 1943:
Italy surrenders to the Allies, but it is not announced to the world until September 8.

September 8, 1943:
Unwilling to let Italy fall entirely to the Allies after its surrender, German troops seize control of northern and central Italy, disarming Italian troops and taking their supplies.

"Hold them by the nose and kick them in the rear," U.S. General George S. Patton often declared. In March 1943, Patton arrived in North Africa to take command of the 2nd Army Corps following its demoralizing defeat at Kasserine Pass in Tunisia. Having led a tank brigade in World War I, Patton championed the use of armored units and provided a powerful counter to the successes of Rommel's panzer lines. From North Africa to Sicily to France, Patton led Allied forces to victories that hastened Germany's retreat. Perhaps more than his battlefield leadership, Patton is remembered for his volcanic temper, flamboyance, and self-confidence, perhaps best exemplified by the twin ivory-handled six-shooters he wore on his hips with his uniform. Patton's swagger, though, got him into trouble. On more than one occasion, he assaulted his troops in the hopes of encouraging them to buck up and work harder. General Dwight D. Eisenhower even temporarily removed him from command after Patton abused wounded soldiers in a field hospital. Shortly after the war, Patton died from injuries he suffered in an automobile accident in December 1945.

SOUTHERN ITALY, 1944
Allied Invasion of Italy and
Operations to 25 September 1943
German Delaying Positions

CAIRO-TEHRAN CONFERENCES

The Cairo-Tehran Conferences were a series of diplomatic meetings in November–December 1943, in which Allied leaders planned for the invasion of Normandy, France, and began to envision the structure of postwar Europe. In the first Cairo, Egypt, Conference on November 23 to 26, 1943, code-named Sextant, Roosevelt, Churchill, and Chinese Nationalist leader Chiang Kai-Shek strategized the war in East Asia.

The Tehran, Persia (Iran), Conference of November 28 to December 1, 1943, code-named Eureka, featured the first joint meeting between the big three Allied leaders: Churchill, Stalin, and Roosevelt. (Churchill and Roosevelt had met on several prior occasions but never with the Soviet premier.) They announced plans for the Normandy invasion, Operation Overlord, tentatively scheduled for May 1944. In their discussions of postwar Europe, the three leaders also began to devise the policy that divided Germany, with its regions separately administered by the Allied powers.

After completing their meetings with Stalin in Tehran, Churchill and Roosevelt returned to Cairo from December 3 to 7, 1943, to encourage Turkish President Ismet Inönü to join the Allies. Desperate to avoid the destruction the Ottoman Empire suffered during the First World War, Inönü maintained Turkey's neutrality.

century. Mistakenly assuming that German forces had taken defensive positions in the monastery, the controversial attack killed civilians who had taken refuge there.

The Italian campaign became a war of attrition that lasted until May 2, 1945, resulting in more than 300,000 Allied casualties and more than 400,000 German casualties. The slow but steady advance of Allied troops in Italy in 1944 further isolated Germany and drained resources strained in the Soviet Union and France. These losses set the stage for a multipronged Allied invasion of German-held Central and Western Europe, with Soviet forces advancing from the east and U.S. and British troops arriving from the west. ✪

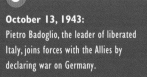

October 13, 1943:
Pietro Badoglio, the leader of liberated Italy, joins forces with the Allies by declaring war on Germany.

November 18, 1943:
The RAF Berlin raids begin with intensive bombing of the city.

D-Day

D-Day stands as the iconic symbol of Allied resolve during World War II. The invasion of German-occupied northern France, on June 6, 1944, provided a critical western battle-front that aided Soviet advances in Eastern Europe and hastened the liberation of France.

Although German commanders had long expected an invasion of France from the English Channel, defensive planning nevertheless proved difficult. With attack possible anywhere along a coast several hundred miles long, Hitler decided to keep most of his forces inland so they could respond directly to wherever the invasion actually occurred. This decision thinned German defenses just enough to make Operation Overlord (as the Allies code-named the invasion) possible. In fact, the Allies prepared several fake invasions to further confuse the Wehrmacht and open a gap for D-Day forces to penetrate. Rommel directed German defenses, which numbered half a million throughout northern France, but Hitler denied his requests to concentrate these forces to repel an amphibious invasion. Even after Allied troops began to land on D-Day, Hitler continued to hold back the bulk of his reinforcements, believing that the actual invasion would come later at a different location.

The Allies' massive preparations included two months of bombing along the Normandy coast, with more than 200,000 missions flown to weaken German defenses. Allied generals codenamed the five beaches where their amphibious forces would strike: Utah, Omaha, Gold, Juno, and Sword.

June 6, 1944:
D-Day. Allied troops storm five beaches in Normandy, France, with 175,000 troops, 600 warships, and almost 10,000 bombers and aircraft.

American assault troops in a landing craft near a beachhead in northern France. The landing is supported by naval gunfire.

June 22, 1944:
President Roosevelt signs the GI Bill of Rights, which promises low-interest home loans and educational benefits to veterans returning from the war.

July 17, 1944:
The Red Army enters Nazi-controlled Poland.

British forces would target Gold and Sword, Canadian troops would attack Juno, and U.S. forces would land at Utah and Omaha. With thousands of paratroopers scheduled to land on either side of the beaches, as well as behind German lines, strategists hoped that the invasion would enable the Allies to gain a toehold in Normandy. From there, they would sweep south and then eastward through France.

In the early-morning hours of June 6, 1944, more than 20,000 Allied paratroopers landed near the beaches in advance of the amphibious assault forces that arrived at sunrise. More than a thousand naval ships and 11,500 aircraft joined the attack. Allied troops, particularly American soldiers who landed at Utah and Omaha beaches, faced terrible losses. German machine gunners held higher ground across the beaches, and they targeted the slow-moving troops who waded onshore and then trudged without defensive cover across open, mine-filled beaches. By the end of the day, more than 150,000 Allied troops had landed but at a cost of more than 10,000 casualties, including 2,000 American dead and wounded at "Bloody Omaha" alone.

Despite such losses, the D-Day assault was a resounding victory and provided the critical station necessary to continue Operation Overlord into France. By the end of the week, 325,000 Allied troops had landed, and by the end of the month, more than a million. More than four years after German troops marched onto the Champs-Élysées, Allied forces liberated Paris on August 25, 1944. The Normandy invasion, combined with Soviet victories in the east, effectively surrounded German forces in Europe. The coming months saw a steady shrinkage of Nazi-controlled territory in Europe as the Wehrmacht retreated on all fronts. ⊙

1. A massive landing and deployment of U.S. troops, supplies, and equipment arrive on Omaha Beach, the day after victorious D-Day action. Barrage balloons keep watch overhead for German aircraft while scores of ships unload men and materials.
2. The Invasion and Opperations, Normandy. 1944
3. Medics helping injured soldier in France. 1944

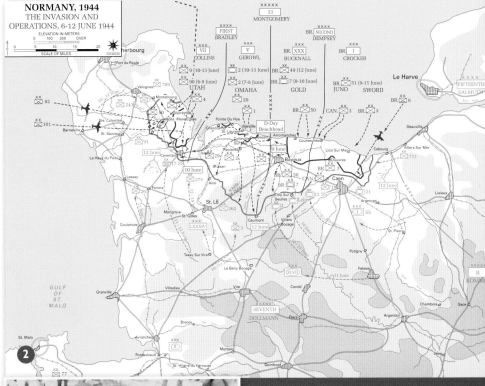

NORMANY, 1944
THE INVASION AND OPERATIONS, 6-12 JUNE 1944

MEDICS

Throughout the Second World War, medical personnel served at the front lines, accompanying advancing troops with little protection for themselves, as hospital units followed to provide necessary surgical care. In addition to treating battle trauma cases, medics treated millions of patients suffering from various diseases and non-battle-related injuries. Advances in medical technology, communication, and transportation enabled World War II medics to excel at their profession, reducing mortality rates to unprecedented low figures. Given the perils of their duties, U.S. medical staff suffered along with their brothers in arms, losing 2,763 personnel and suffering 11,826 wounded.

On D-Day, medics parachuted into Nazi-occupied France along with the 82nd and 101st Airborne Divisions and landed on Omaha and Utah beaches with amphibious assault forces. Medical personnel operated continuous service across the English Channel, transporting thousands of wounded soldiers to treatment centers safely away from the front lines. With the success of Operation Overlord, medics continued eastward toward Germany, as Allied forces continued on to Berlin. By the end of the war, more than a quarter of a million medics worked alongside three million U.S. troops stationed in Europe.

July 21, 1944:
U.S. Marines and Army take back control of the island of Guam from the Japanese.

July 24, 1944:
For the first time, the world sees the Nazis' plan for the Jewish people, when the Red Army liberates the Majdanek concentration camp in Poland.

Polish prisoners in striped uniforms stand in rows before Nazi officers at the Buchenwald Concentration Camp, Weimar, Germany, ca 1943.

August 4, 1944:
Jewish teenager Anne Frank and her family are arrested by German police after hiding in an Amsterdam attic.

August 21, 1944:
Members of the Dumbarton Oaks Conference plan the framework of the United Nations over a six-week period of time.

The Holocaust

Given the spans of time and place that distance our world from that of the Second World War, it's difficult to imagine the horrors of the Holocaust. The actual term emerged after the war, as a means of conveying the all-encompassing devastation Nazi Germany and the Axis powers wrought upon Jewish populations in Europe.

1. Children stand behind a barbed wire fence at the Nazi concentration camp at Auschwitz in southern Poland.
2. Onlookers stare at smashed Jewish shop window following riots of the night of November 9th in Berlin. November 10, 1938
3. Anne Frank
4. A Jewish family wears the Star of David to indicate that they are Jews, a commonplace sight in Germany after Kristallnacht. ca 1938

The events that came to be known as the Holocaust evolved from a steady stream of anti-Semitic (anti-Jewish) policies instituted by the Nazi regime during the 1930s. Adolf Hitler rose to power by blaming Jews for Germany's downfall after World War I. As chancellor, he crafted policies that isolated Jewish Germans from German society, revoked their status as citizens (Nuremberg Laws), and continued to single out Jews as the cause of all of the nation's problems. These measures essentially made Jews part of an underclass, without the rights and powers of other Germans.

These policies inflamed anti-Semitic (anti-Jewish) hatred and led to a series of attacks on Jews throughout Germany. On November 9, 1938, the Nazis encouraged anti-Jewish raids across Germany. *Kristallnacht*, or the "Night of Broken Glass," saw countless acts of vandalism against Jewish-owned businesses and places of worship. The German government arrested more than 30,000 Jewish men and killed nearly one hundred others, 1,000 synagogues were vandalized, and more than 7,500 Jewish-owned shops were looted. During the war, these policies turned to outright murder with the creation of concentration/extermination camps.

In the early stages of the war, the Nazis required that every Jew wear a yellow Star of David patch and forced them to live in urban ghettos, further separating Jews from the rest of the country.

Years of attacks, discrimination, and political scapegoating culminated in the extermination policies of the war era. Beginning with Operation Barbarossa, the German invasion of the Soviet Union in 1941, German troops targeted Jews throughout Eastern Europe. Mobile killing squads, called *Einsatzgruppen*, followed advancing Nazi troops and systematically slaughtered any Jews they encountered. The Einsatzgruppen destroyed entire cities with large Jewish populations.

On January 20, 1942, at the Wannsee Conference in Berlin, Nazi leaders planned what they termed the "Final Solution." This policy called for the extermination camps soon constructed throughout Axis-controlled Europe. Seeking the total annihilation of Jews throughout Europe, the Nazis devoted enormous wartime resources

August 25, 1944:
The Allies liberate Paris from the Nazis.

August 26, 1944:
German forces withdraw from Greece.

October 2, 1944:
The Allies enter Germany from the north and face resistance from German troops at the Siegfried Line—the fortification along the western border of Germany.

to constructing a transportation network that would take millions of Jews to their deaths.

In addition to the concentration camps already developed to imprison political prisoners since the early 1930s, the Nazis built extermination camps whose sole purpose was mass murder. Unspeakable horrors occurred daily in the camps, with torture, rape, disease, executions, forced labor, gas chambers, and so-called medical experiments among innumerable other atrocities.

As the German military suffered defeats to Allied forces in the latter months of the war, the Nazi leadership actually increased the death rates at the camps. By the war's end, more than six million Jews, roughly two-thirds of Europe's Jewish population at the start of the conflict, had been killed. At least an equal number of non-Jews died in the Nazi death camps. ✪

ANNE FRANK

Millions of people throughout the world have learned about the Holocaust through the diary of one of its victims, Anne Frank. On her thirteenth birthday, in 1942, Anne received a diary as a present from her parents. For the next two years, she filled its pages with her thoughts about her family, her life as a teenager, and her experiences as a Jew living in the German-occupied city of Amsterdam, in the Netherlands.

Having fled their German homeland to avoid Nazi rule, the Frank family decided to go into hiding in Amsterdam when German troops marched into the city in May 1940. The family lived for four years in a set of secret rooms in a part of the building where Anne's father had worked. The Franks, along with four other people, needed to stay absolutely silent during the day and could not go outside at any time. On page after page of her diary, Anne detailed what news she learned of the outside world—reports of concentration camps and the mass murder of Jews and families separated. As noted in Anne's final diary entry, Nazi police discovered the Franks on August 4, 1944. The family was separated at the camp at Auschwitz-Birkenau and later Anne and her sister, Margot, were transferred to the Bergen-Belsen camp. The sisters died there of typhus in March 1945. Anne's father, Otto, was the family's only survivor. Friends kept Anne's diary safe until after the war. He published it in 1947 with the title *Het Achterhuis* or *The Secret Annex*. In 1952, the English translation was published with the title, *The Diary of a Young Girl*. Since its publication, Anne's diary has sold more than thirty million copies and been translated into more than sixty-five languages. The building where the Frank family hid is now a museum in Amsterdam.

October 18, 1944:
The Japanese initiate Operation Victory (*Sho-Go*) in a frantic attempt to keep Allied troops off the islands of Japan.

October 20, 1944:
American troops land on the island of Leyte in the Philippines to take back land the Japanese had claimed more than two years earlier.

October 21, 1944:
German forces, beaten down by Allied attacks, surrender the city of Aachen. This will be the first German city to fall.

The Battle of the Bulge

The Battle of the Bulge refers to the last-ditch German counter offensive against U.S. and British forces in December 1944. The German counterattack followed months of steady Allied advances after the D-Day invasion of Normandy, France. Allied troops moved steadily through France, Belgium, and the Netherlands in the summer of 1944 and then prepared for entry into Germany itself.

With the aid of General Patton's tank battalions, General Eisenhower regrouped Allied forces throughout Western Europe and successfully continued the march into Germany. Faced with dwindling options, Hitler decided that his only option for success would be to divide the Allied armies arriving from the west. He sought to split the British and American troops and race his forces to capture the port city of Antwerp, Belgium. The strategy had little chance of success, but Hitler devoted the remnants of his Wehrmacht to it with devastating consequences.

On December 16, 1944, in the dense, snow-blanketed Ardennes forests of Belgium, thousands of German tanks rolled westward without warning. Surprising the Allied troops stationed in the area, the German lines moved forward rapidly, creating a bulge in the Allied armies that expanded for dozens of miles. The Wehrmacht even sent English-speaking troops to the front lines to confuse Allied soldiers, who couldn't tell whether they were speaking with friend or foe. In total, U.S. troops suffered greater losses in the Battle of the Bulge than in any other engagement during the war: More than 10,000 killed, 50,000 wounded, and more than 20,000 POWs. In Malmedy, Belgium, German troops massacred nearly one hundred American prisoners, in an act that would be investigated as a war crime following the conflict.

And yet, the Allied lines held. At Bastogne, within the Bulge, American forces with the 101st and 82nd Airborne Divisions managed to repel capture but remained under siege for days. Patton recognized the necessity of reaching these men and sped his troops there as quickly as possible. Patton's troops arrived the day after Christmas and turned the tide of the battle. These forces included two thousand African-American soldiers, who had been reassigned to combat duty because of heavy losses during the initial assault. In January, Allied forces continued to reduce the bulge and completely repulsed the attack by the end of the month. Hitler's plan to divide the U.S. and British forces had failed. The Wehrmacht suffered more than 100,000 casualties, a blow from which Germany did not recover. ✪

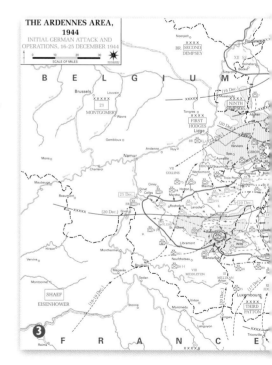

THE ARDENNES AREA, 1944
INITIAL GERMAN ATTACK AND OPERATIONS, 16-25 DECEMBER 1944

November 7, 1944:
Franklin D. Roosevelt defeats Thomas E. Dewey in the race for U.S. president and begins his fourth consecutive term.

November 26, 1944:
To hide evidence of the Nazis' crimes, SS commander Heinrich Himmler orders the destruction of Auschwitz's gas chambers and crematoria.

An oven at Auschwitz concentration camp, Poland. The ovens were primarily used to incinerate the corpses of those inmates who were executed in gas chambers.

1. Vehicles and infantry of the US 1st Army on the road during winter fighting in the Ardennes forest conflict known as the Battle of the Bulge.
2. Smoke rises from debris-strewn buildings in Bastogne during the Battle of the Bulge.
3. The Ardennes Area. 1944
4. Cpl. Carlton Chapman, a machine-gunner in an M-4 tank, attached to a Motor Transport unit near Nancy, France. November 5, 1944
5. View of Bastogne, including *Nuts* on signs of WWII landmarks.
6. Pilots discuss the day's exploits at a U.S. base in the Mediterranean theater. They were part of a U.S. Army Air Forces fighter squadron credited with shooting down 8 of the 28 German planes destroyed in dogfights over the new Allied beachheads south of Rome on January 27, 1944

Despite segregation and racial inequality in the United States, African-Americans volunteered for the military services by the hundreds of thousands. *The Pittsburgh Courier*, one of the country's most influential African-American newspapers, endorsed a "Double-V" campaign for the war—victory abroad against the Axis and victory at home against racism. Proponents hoped that by demonstrating their loyalty to the U.S. in the war effort, African-Americans would gain civil rights when black soldiers returned home victorious.

Overall, 1.1 million African-Americans served during the war, with nearly half that number stationed abroad. They fought in Europe and the Pacific respectively, but served in segregated divisions and were often held back from combat duty. When the Battle of the Bulge threatened U.S. forces in Europe in 1944–5, General Patton used integrated forces to counterattack advancing German lines. The battalion broke the Siegfried Line (German Western Wall), allowing Patton's army to move into Germany. The most famous African-American outfit of World War II was the 332nd Fighter Group, known as the Tuskegee Airmen, who led hundreds of bombing missions over Germany. Due to these successes and growing campaigns for civil rights after the war, President Truman signed Executive Order 9981 in 1948, which integrated all branches of the U.S. Armed Services.

"Nuts!"

—Major General Anthony McAuliffe's one-word response to Germany's demand for the surrender of his 101st Airborne Division in Bastogne, Belgium

December 16, 1944:
The Battle of the Bulge begins as German forces attack U.S. strongholds in the dense, snow-covered Ardennes forest—Hitler's last major offensive.

January 25, 1945:
The Battle of the Bulge concludes with the Allies being victorious.

Members of the U.S. 1st Army guarding German prisoners, captured during winter fighting in the Ardennes forest known as the Battle of the Bulge.

Island-Hopping Toward Japan

The Allied victory at Guadalcanal in 1943 changed the dynamic of the Pacific war. Now possessing a stronger naval fleet, Allied commanders planned to steadily make their way toward Japan by capturing key islands en route and avoiding others. Japanese defenses were often dug into heavily fortified positions, often aided by natural features such as caves and cliffs. But they were increasingly outnumbered, lacked reinforcements, and did not possess the firepower waged against them by Allied troops from land, sea, and air. The Allies, comprised primarily of United States naval forces, hoped to avoid as many of these engagements as possible, instead working to cut off certain islands where Japanese forces had become entrenched, isolate those enclaves, and then cut them off from their supply routes. This "island-hopping" campaign, as it came to be known, featured devastating battles, acts of unspeakable brutality, and a war of attrition that gradually diminished Japanese forces.

At the island of Saipan, on June 15, 1944, U.S. Marines conducted an amphibious assault that evolved into a weeks-long battle with well-defended Japanese troops. As their defensive lines began to fail, Japanese troops conducted hopeless charges toward Allied positions. Thousands of other Japanese troops and civilians committed suicide rather than be taken prisoner. Three thousand Marines died during the engagement, but Japanese losses came to more than 27,000. The victory at Saipan provided the Allies with a base for long-range bombing missions over Japan and a staging ground for an invasion of the Philippines. Moreover, battles of attrition such as on Saipan favored American forces, which possessed more weaponry, better supplies, and cover fire from air and sea. Fighting at Guam and Tinian produced similar results, with victories for the Allies and terrible defeats for Japan.

At the Battle of Leyte Gulf in the Philippines in October 1944, the U.S. Navy achieved perhaps its greatest victory in the Pacific. Despite the loss of three aircraft carriers and 2,000 sailors, the United States fleet destroyed four Japanese carriers and more than twenty other warships. The defeat crippled the Japanese fleet, whose commanders began using kamikaze squadrons as last, desperate measures to strike American ships. In another month-long island

January 17, 1945:
The Red Army frees the capital city of Warsaw and continues their advance to Germany through Poland.

January 27, 1945:
The Soviet army liberates Auschwitz. The Nazis marched 70,000 prisoners from the camp the week before, but nearly 7,700 weak, starving prisoners remained.

February 4–11:
Allied leaders Roosevelt, Churchill, and Stalin meet at Yalta (in modern-day Ukraine) to discuss how to rebuild Europe when the war is over.

February 13, 1945:
The Soviets take Budapest, Hungary.

engagement in February to March 1945, U.S. forces captured Iwo Jima and continued their approach to the main islands of Japan. On February 23, Marines captured Mount Suribachi, which overlooked the island. The photograph of five soldiers raising the American flag atop the mountain became one of the iconic images of the war. The picture also helped rejuvenate support for the war effort at home, which had diminished somewhat amid heavy losses in Europe and the Pacific.

The invasion of Okinawa from April to June 1945 brought a horrible conclusion to the island campaign. Situated only 350 miles from Japan, Okinawa held out as the last hope for Japan's defense against advancing Allied forces. More than 200,000 U.S. personnel participated in the invasion, more than double the troops on the other side. More than 12,000 Americans died during the battle, by far the most losses suffered by the United States in the Pacific. But nearly all of the Japanese soldiers on the island died in battle or by suicide. Moreover, the clash brought a horrible civilian toll, as thousands of Okinawans committed suicide or were killed by Japanese soldiers who refused to let them be taken captive. Faced with news of these horrors, American officials, military strategists, and the public at large worried about the sacrifices that would be necessary to bring Japan's surrender. ✪

5

KAMIKAZE PILOTS

Faced with mounting defeats against a better-equipped American foe, kamikaze suicide fliers offered a terrifying means to attempt to counter the increasingly dire tenor of the Pacific war. Translated as "divine wind," the word *kamikaze* harkened back to the legendary typhoon that decimated an invading force set to conquer Japan in the thirteenth century. Desperation fueled the decision by Japanese commanders to create kamikaze fighter squadrons, whose pilots promised their lives in return for the glory of dying in battle. The kamikaze became an official strategy on October 19, 1944, and its first use occurred within a matter of days during the disastrous Battle of the Leyte Gulf, in the Philippines. Suicide pilots deliberately flew their planes into Allied ships, particularly aircraft carriers, as a last-ditch attempt to turn the conflict's tide. As American forces advanced closer and closer to Japan, the deployment of kamikaze increased precipitously. By the end of the war, 5,000 kamikaze pilots had died in battle, having destroyed dozens of enemy warships.

1. A marine aims at a Japanese sniper on Okinawa. June 22, 1945
2. A formidable task force carves out a beachhead, about 350 miles from the Japanese mainland. Landing craft of all kinds blacken the sea out to the horizon, where stand the battlewagons, cruisers, and destroyers. Okinawa. April 13, 1945
3. Marines use every available means of transporting supplies to the front lines on Saipan. ca June 1944
4. Corsair fighter looses its load of rocket projectiles on a run against a Japanese stronghold on Okinawa. ca. June 1945
5. The Pacific Theater. 1941
6. *Kamikaze* (Divine Wind) pilots, who deliberately crash their bomb-laden planes onto American warships during World War II. They have already tied on the honorary ribbons that they always wore when they were about to go on a mission.

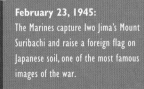

February 13–15, 1945:
Allied aircraft carry out a series of intense bombings on the German city of Dresden, causing firestorms that destroy the city, killing nearly 30,000 people.

February 19, 1945:
U.S. Marines storm the beaches of Iwo Jima, setting off one of the deadliest battles of the war in the Pacific.

February 23, 1945:
The Marines capture Iwo Jima's Mount Suribachi and raise a foreign flag on Japanese soil, one of the most famous images of the war.

The Allies in Germany

Germany's defeat at the Battle of the Bulge in January 1945 marked the last of its grand offensive maneuvers. With clear flight paths over most of Germany, the Allied bombers attacked cities throughout the country. Hoping to weaken popular support for the war effort and spur surrender by the Nazi leadership, the Allies targeted civilian populations with massive air raids. The assault on Dresden in February 1945 killed as many as 50,000 people and destroyed much of the historic city. Although in retreat, the remnants of the Wehrmacht continued to fight.

Following their victory in the Ardennes campaign, Allied troops advanced swiftly through Belgium toward Germany. Once at the German border, they faced the Siegfried Line, or West Wall. These defensive fortifications spanned 300 miles and provided one final challenge to Allied soldiers attempting to enter Germany from the west. On March 7, 1945, Allied forces crossed the Rhine River into Germany at the town of Remagen. Hitler had ordered the bridge at Remagen destroyed and when the Allies captured it, the officer responsible for its destruction was executed. Before the bridge finally collapsed, the Allies had poured thousands of troops and armored weaponry into Germany.

Surrounded, the Nazis also faced massive armies arriving from the east, as Soviet forces swept through Poland and into eastern Germany. Soviet forces marched through Poland and the other Eastern European nations formerly conquered by the Nazis, including Hungary, Austria, and Czechoslovakia. The coming months saw Allied forces advance into Germany from all fronts, encircling the capital of Berlin and preparing a final siege to end the war in Europe.

As Allied troops moved into formerly German-controlled territory, they encountered the aftermath of the Nazis' Final Solution. Soviet forces liberated the first concentration camp at Majdanek, Poland, in July 1944. In January 1945, the Auschwitz-Birkenau death camp was taken. For many soldiers, the scenes of devastation and suffering they witnessed could not be adequately described. Upon reaching the camps in April 1945, General Eisenhower saw piles of dead bodies and met

March 7, 1945:
The first Allied forces cross the Rhine River at Remagen, Germany, and advance farther into the center of the country.

March 9–10, 1945:
The United States attacks Tokyo with incendiary (fire) bombs, resulting in a firestorm that kills more than 100,000 and leaves one million people homeless.

April 1, 1945:
U.S. Marines land on Okinawa in the largest invasion of the Pacific war.

YALTA CONFERENCE

In February 1945, the Big Three Allied leaders—Roosevelt, Churchill, and Stalin—met for the final time in Yalta. They decided that Germany would be punished economically and divided into four separate zones that would be governed temporarily by the Allied powers of France, Britain, the United States, and the Soviet Union. The Soviet Union, which had essentially taken over the Eastern Europe countries that had been controlled by the Axis, agreed to allow free and open elections in those nations after the war. (Stalin's failure to live up to this part of the agreement would become one of the defining issues of the Cold War.) In addition to pondering the future of Europe and Asia, the leaders finalized plans for a United Nations, modeled on the League of Nations that emerged after the First World War. With Roosevelt's health worsening, and Churchill losing his position and being replaced during the conference, Stalin left Yalta in the strongest position. His diplomatic victories there set the Soviet Union on a path to challenge the U.S. as the world's superpower during the postwar era.

hundreds of emaciated survivors. He implored his troops to see the camps to understand the true nature of their cause. He sent the following message back to the United States "From my own personal observation, I can state unequivocally that all written statements up to now do not paint the full horrors." Only with these encounters did the Allies begin to fully comprehend the toll wrought by the Nazi regime upon the peoples of Europe. ✪

1. Liberated prisoners in the Mauthausen concentration camp near Linz, Austria, give rousing welcome to cavalrymen of the 11th Armored Division. The banner across the wall was made by Spanish Loyalist prisoners. May 6, 1945
2. Allied troops advance into Germany, through the Siegfried Line. ca. 1945
3. Franklin D. Roosevelt, Churchill, and Stalin at the Livadia Palace in Yalta., February 2, 1945
4. Allied Occupation Zones, Central Europe. 1944

HITLER'S "UNDESIRABLES"

In addition to the six million Jews killed during the Holocaust, there were many non-Jewish civilians who died at the hands of Nazi soldiers during Hitler's twelve-year reign. The first concentration camps, built shortly after his rise to power in 1933, held political prisoners that included socialists, communists, and other activists deemed threats to Nazi rule. In the years leading up to and including the war, these forced labor camps expanded to contain millions of so-called "undesirables": Jews, Gypsies, Jehovah's Witnesses, homosexuals, the disabled and infirm, clergy members, academics, economic elites, and millions of Soviet prisoners of war. In addition, the Einsatzgruppen (mobile killing squads) annihilated entire towns throughout Eastern Europe. From Operation Barbarossa through the Final Solution, the German military massacred twelve to seventeen million people in extermination camps and in attacks on civilian populations throughout Eastern Europe.

April 12, 1945:
President Roosevelt has a stroke and dies later that day. Vice President Harry Truman is sworn in as President of the United States.

Harry S. Truman takes the oath at the start of his term of office as the 33rd president of the United States. Standing beside him are his wife Bess and daughter Margaret.

April 13, 1945:
The Red Army captures the Austrian capital of Vienna.

April 28, 1945:
Benito Mussolini is executed along with fifteen other leaders of the Italian Social Republic.

Victory in Europe

Surrounded on all fronts by advancing Allied forces, the Nazi high command retreated to bunkers within the city of Berlin. Hitler delivered his final radio address in January 1945, and then moved underground to spend the ensuing months listening to the relentless explosions of enemy shells pummeling the city above. As Allied shelling gradually reduced the German capital to rubble, the Führer likely had time to contemplate the dramatic reversal of fortune his Nazi Party had experienced during its fifteen horrific years in power. In the early months of 1945, as Allied tanks and planes steadily decimated Germany, the country experienced firsthand the devastation it had wrought upon the peoples of Europe.

1. Ecstatic crowds celebrate V-E Day in London's Piccadilly Square, at the end of World War II. May 8, 1945
2. British Prime Minister Winston Churchill gives the famous V sign (victory sign) to large crowds gathered in Whitehall and Parliament Square from the balcony of the Ministry of Health on the evening of VE Day. London, England. May 8, 1945
3. Allied leaders at the signing of the document of unconditional surrender. May 7, 1945
4. Enormous crowds celebrate VE Day in Times Square, New York. Servicemen and civilians wave flags and newspapers with headlines announcing the event.
5. President Franklin D. Roosevelt's funeral cortege. 1945

As U.S. and British armies advanced from the west, Soviet forces moved through formerly Nazi-occupied capitals of Eastern Europe, taking Warsaw, Poland, in January, Budapest, Hungary, in February, and Vienna, Austria, in April. General Eisenhower's troops stopped fifty miles from Berlin, while more than two million Soviet soldiers moved into the city in April. Nazi leaders continued the fight, conscripting young boys and elderly men to die in the final throes of Nazi rule. Blaming everyone in Germany but himself for his nation's defeat, Hitler committed suicide on April 30, 1945, in his bunker in Berlin. Only a few days later, Soviet forces captured the city. The remains of Hitler's body have never been recovered.

Two days earlier, on April 28, Benito Mussolini was executed by his Italian captors. The following day, the commander of Axis troops in Italy surrendered to the Allies. Finally, on May 7, General Alfred Jodl surrendered the remaining German forces to Allied commanders. This act ended the war in Europe and sparked massive celebrations on both sides of the Atlantic. President Truman proclaimed that day of rejoicing, May 8, V-E (Victory in Europe) Day.

The war's conclusion in Europe raised many of the controversial questions that the victors faced following World War I. To what extent would Germany be punished for the war? Would Germany be allowed to rebuild? How would the nation itself be governed and would it be occupied by the Allies? The Big Three

April 29, 1945:
Italy surrenders to the Allies.

April 30, 1945:
Hitler commits suicide in his bunker in Berlin.

May 2, 1945:
The Soviets seize Berlin.

leaders had reached tentative agreements on these issues at the Yalta Conference earlier that year but, with Roosevelt and Churchill no longer in power, how would the Allies proceed? In the days and weeks after V-E Day, France, Britain, the United States, and the Soviet Union partitioned Germany into four zones of occupation. But the emerging Cold War between the United States and the Soviet Union quickly brought tension to postwar Europe. Throughout Eastern Europe, Soviet troops remained after defeating German occupiers, installing their own regimes in place of those controlled by the Nazis. Having just suffered through years of turmoil, death, and devastation, Europeans prepared themselves for another possible global conflict. As this new Cold War brewed in Europe, the United States concentrated its military might on defeating the last remaining Axis foe—Japan. ✪

ROOSEVELT DIES

On April 12, 1945, President Franklin Delano Roosevelt died from a cerebral hemorrhage at his "Little White House" in Warm Springs, Georgia. Roosevelt's death shocked and saddened the country, sparking a national outpouring of grief. First elected in 1932, Roosevelt won reelection three times and served as president longer than anyone before or since. His leadership through two of the nation's greatest crises—the Great Depression and World War II—made Roosevelt a powerful and popular president.

For the first time in more than twelve years, Americans had a new president. While the war appeared to be winding down in Europe, much needed to be accomplished in Europe and the Pacific. When Eleanor Roosevelt informed Vice President Harry Truman that the president had died, Truman offered his condolences and asked if there was anything he could do to help. Eleanor replied, "Is there anything we can do for you, for you are the one in trouble now." As Truman later recalled about his becoming president in the midst of war, "I felt like the moon, the stars, and all the planets had fallen on me." Roosevelt's body was taken by train to Washington, D.C., and then to its final resting place at his home in Hyde Park, New York.

May 7, 1945:
On behalf of all the German forces, General Alfred Jodl surrenders unconditionally to the Allies.

General Alfred Jodl signs the document of unconditional surrender. On Jodl's left is General Admiral von Friedeburg of the German Navy, and on the right is Major Wilhelm Oxenius of the German General Staff. Behind von Friedeburg is Maj. Gen. K. W. D. Strong, G-2, SHAEF. May 7, 1945

May 8, 1945:
President Truman declares this Victory in Europe (V-E) Day.

June 26, 1945:
The Charter of the United Nations is signed by fifty countries in San Francisco.

Victory in Japan

On the evening of March 9, 1945, residents of Tokyo, Japan, saw their city engulfed in flames. Thousands of American bombers dropped incendiary bombs throughout the city. These devices ignited when detonated, spreading fires throughout the city, whose structures were primarily built from wood. Within twelve hours, more than 100,000 Japanese had been killed and 90 percent of Tokyo's residents—more than one million people—lost their homes. The firebombing of Tokyo occurred as U.S. forces completed their island-hopping campaign through the Pacific and prepared for a full-scale invasion of Japan. As losses mounted in Japan, American commanders feared the death toll that would accompany such a land assault. U.S. government officials searched for a means of ending the war quickly and avoiding the battles of attrition that had plagued the Pacific campaign.

1. The mushroom-shaped cloud following the dropping of the A-Bomb on the Japanese city of Hiroshima.

2. Some of the devastation after the American A-bomb attack on Hiroshima, Japan. September 1945

3. Col. Paul W. Tibbets, Jr., pilot of the Enola Gay, the plane that dropped the atomic bomb on Hiroshima, waves from his cockpit before the takeoff. August 6, 1945

4. Sir Arthur Percival and Jonathan Wainwright salute General Douglas MacArthur as Supreme Commander of the Allied Forces just before he accepts the Japanese unconditional surrender document. Mamoru Shigemitsu, the top-hatted foreign minister, along with General Yoshijiro Umezo, the army chief of staff, lead the Japanese delegaation, on board the USS *Missouri* in Tokyo Bay. September 2, 1945

5. Japanese Rear Admiral Isoroku Yamamoto, commander and architect of the Japanese attack on Pearl Harbor. ca 1937

The answer to these concerns came as President Truman met with Soviet Premier Stalin and British Prime Minister Churchill at the Potsdam Conference in July 1945. Following the death of President Roosevelt, and the replacing of Churchill with a new prime minister during the conference, Potsdam signified the beginning of a new era in international affairs. With victory already achieved in Europe, the Allied leaders anticipated a new struggle for global supremacy between the United States and the Soviet Union. Despite the tens of millions of casualties his nation had suffered during the war, Stalin struck an exultant tone over the victories his forces had achieved in Eastern Europe. Truman took a harder line than his predecessor regarding plans for the postwar world order. He expressed concern about Soviet intentions in Eastern Europe and warned that the Soviet Union would attempt to take power in Europe, replacing Germany as the continent's dominant power.

Truman beamed confidently at the outset of the conference, as he learned that the Manhattan Project

was a success. On July 16, the day before the Potsdam meetings began, the U.S. military detonated the first atomic weapon in human history. The so-called Trinity test in Alamogordo, New Mexico, produced an explosion with the force of 20,000 tons of TNT. Truman concluded that this weapon could swiftly end the war with Japan and provide the foundation for American global supremacy after the war.

Following the Trinity test, Truman and his military advisors determined to manufacture and drop atomic weapons on Japan as soon as they were completed. Faced with the decision of where to deploy these nuclear bombs, strategists ruled out the ancient capital of Kyoto because of its historical significance. They opted instead for Hiroshima, primarily because it had suffered relatively minor damage from U.S. air raids. Officials concluded that the city's status would enable scientists to better gauge the bomb's destructive capacity.

On August 6, 1945, the U.S. bomber *Enola Gay* flew toward its target without fighter escort. The bomber passed through Japanese air defenses without incident

July 17–August 2, 1945: Truman, Churchill, and Stalin meet at the Potsdam Conference to discuss the status of postwar Europe and the continuing war with Japan.

July 26, 1945: The Allies formally warn Japan that they will face heavier attacks if they do not surrender unconditionally.

August 6, 1945: The U.S. military drops an atomic bomb on the Japanese city of Hiroshima, killing approximately 80,000 civilians.

> "We call upon the Government of Japan to proclaim now the unconditional surrender of all the Japanese armed forces. . . . The alternative for Japan is prompt and utter destruction."
>
> —*Potsdam Declaration, issued by Allied leaders, July 26, 1945*

and dropped its payload. At 8:15 a.m., a searing flash of light appeared over the skies of Hiroshima, followed by a massive fireball that destroyed virtually the entire city. Exploding 2,000 feet over the city center, the bomb unleashed the force of 12,000 tons of TNT, leveling all buildings in its vicinity and killing 80,000 people within moments. Tens of thousands more soon died from burns and radiation poisoning.

Two days later, the Soviet Union officially declared war against Japan. Then, on August 9, the United States dropped another atomic bomb on Nagasaki. The second attack caused 40,000 immediate deaths and nearly the same number in its aftermath. Though the Nagasaki bomb was more powerful than its predecessor at Hiroshima, it exploded in a mountainous region, with some of its force absorbed by the moun-

tains that surrounded the city.

Shocked by the first attack on Hiroshima, intense debate flared within the Japanese government over whether to surrender. Military hardliners attempted a coup d'etat in their attempt to maintain power and prolong the war. The strategy failed and, with the endorsement of Emperor Hirohito himself, the Japanese government began the process of surrender. ✪

ISOROKU YAMAMOTO

Until his death in 1943, Admiral Isoroku Yamamoto stood as the most popular military figure in Japan during the Second World War. Ironically, Yamamoto had argued against war with the United States, only to find himself the chief strategist for the assault on Pearl Harbor. Having studied at Harvard University and worked in Washington, D.C., following World War I, Yamamoto predicted that a direct confrontation with the United States would result in a terribly costly defeat for Japan. With many of his fellow officers convinced that the U.S. must be attacked to ensure Japan's victory, Yamamoto concluded that a massive, surprise attack on the U.S. Pacific fleet in Hawaii would provide the best chance to bring about a negotiated settlement with the U.S.

Following early Japanese victories, American forces had begun to turn the corner toward the eventual destruction of Japan's military forces, when U.S. intelligence decrypted the admiral's flight plan in the Solomon Islands. After confirming with President Roosevelt that Yamamoto should be targeted, a squad of U.S. Army Air Force fighters successfully attacked Yamamoto's flight group on April 18, 1943, shooting down the admiral's plane. Yamamoto's death resulted in the loss of Japan's greatest military strategist and dealt a severe psychological blow to the Japanese public.

August 8, 1945:
The Soviet Union declares war on Japan.

August 9, 1945:
The U.S. military drops a second atomic bomb on the Japanese city of Nagasaki, killing approximately 40,000 civilians.

August 14, 1945:
President Truman announces Japan's surrender to the Allies, ending World War II, setting off celebrations throughout the U.S. and the world.

The Aftermath

At noon on August 15, 1945, Japanese Emperor Hirohito made a rare public address, broadcast by radio to his citizenry. For nearly everyone listening in Japan, it was the first time they had heard his voice. He announced his nation's surrender to the Allies and the end of the Second World War. The speech touched off massive celebrations throughout the United States and the world, as people poured into city streets to celebrate V-J (Victory over Japan) Day and the war's end. Upon signing the formal surrender agreement aboard the USS *Missouri* on September 2, the United States began its occupation of Japan. General Douglas MacArthur led the six-year occupation, in which the United States directed Japan's reconstruction and invested millions of dollars to rebuild the nation's infrastructure and economy. With tensions rising with the Soviet Union, the United States made Japan, its former enemy, its most important ally in East Asia.

In the Middle East, Jews sought a safe haven following the Holocaust. With aid from the United States and the UN, the new state of Israel was formed in 1948 in what had been Palestine. From across the world, nearly 700,000 Jews immigrated to Israel after its creation. Their new home provided only slight refuge from the battles of the Second World War, as the Arab-Israeli War began shortly after Israel's formation in 1948.

On the American home front, millions of soldiers faced the challenge of returning to their previous lives and responsibilities. The GI Bill of Rights provided crucial assistance for those making the transition to postwar society. The bill, signed into law in 1944, provided returning service members with money for education, low-interest loans to purchase homes, and other benefits to help returning soldiers.

In the months and years following the war, the Allies conducted trials in Europe and Asia to punish war criminals and reveal the extent of Axis atrocities during the conflict. In the famous Nuremberg Trials, twenty-two Nazi leaders stood trial for their role in the Holocaust and numerous other horrific acts during the war. Ultimately, twelve defendants were sentenced to death by hanging. In a larger series of trials that lasted from 1946 until 1949, 185 Nazis stood trial, including concentration camp administrators, SS officers, Einsatzgruppen, and medical doctors who conducted experiments on prisoners. Twenty-four of these defendants were executed and 107 imprisoned. In Japan, twenty-eight Japanese leaders were tried for Class A war crimes,

August 15, 1945:
Emperor Hirohito delivers a radio address to announce that Japan has surrendered to the Allies.

September 2, 1945:
Japan signs an official surrender agreement aboard the USS *Missouri*.

October 24, 1945:
The United Nations Charter is ratified, bringing the organization officially into existence.

50

including Tojo Hideki, who had served as prime minister during the war. Seven of these defendants were sentenced to death. Thousands of other trials were conducted for lower-level officers in the Japanese military, primarily related to their treatment of Allied POWs.

Just as the victors had done during the latter stages of World War I, the Allies created a body to foster international diplomacy rather than war. The United Nations, like the League of Nations before it, was formed with the goal of maintaining world peace and security. Delegates from fifty nations signed the UN charter on June 26, 1945, and its founding charter was formally ratified on October 24 of that year. The founding members of the United Nations hoped to reconstruct the world in a manner that would avoid the disasters that followed the First World War.

Yet the world already faced a Cold War on the horizon. In the latter days of the war, the Soviet Union amassed power in Eastern Europe and developed alliances in East Asia. As in Japan, the United States devoted significant resources to rebuilding Western Europe. From 1948 to 1951, the Marshall Plan provided more than $13 billion in aid to European nations allied with the United States. The money helped reconstruct societies ravaged by war, as well as provided an American counter to Soviet strength in Eastern Europe. Ironically, the Cold War saw former allies become enemies and wartime enemies become the most crucial of allies. ✪

1. Defendants sit in their dock during the Nuremberg Trials. Goering, Hess, von Ribbentrop, and Keitel are in the front row. ca 1945–1946
2. Marshall Plan aid to Germany totaled $1,390,600 and enabled that country to rise from the ashes of defeat, as symbolized by this worker in West Berlin. Even a year before the end of the Marshall Plan in 1951, Germany had surpassed her prewar industrial production level. West Berlin, Germany. ca. 1948–1955
3. The construction of a segment of the Berlin Wall at Stallschreiberstrasse. 1961

THE COLD WAR

Contrary to the goals of the United Nations, World War II's conclusion did not bring international harmony. Rather, the aftermath saw the creation of a new conflict known as the Cold War—a competition for world supremacy between two nations—the United States and the Soviet Union. In the final days of the Second World War, Soviet and U.S. forces scrambled to gain control of Axis-held territory and forge alliances with their former enemies. The Soviet Union replaced Nazi rule in Eastern Europe with its own authority. Survivors of the German invasion in Czechoslovakia, Poland, Hungary, and other nations witnessed new regimes created that were allied with, or directly controlled by, the Soviet Union. Germany, initially divided into four parts after the war, merged into two nations—East and West Germany—East Germany allied with the Soviet Union and West Germany with the U.S. A similar division occurred in East Asia, as the U.S. occupied Japan after V-J Day. North and South Korea formed, with the northern half of the Korean peninsula supported by the Soviet Union and the southern half by the U.S. With the Soviet Union's development of nuclear weaponry in 1949, the world entered a new phase of tension and strife that continued for forty years. The conflict was called the Cold War because U.S. and Soviet forces never met on the battlefield.

November 20, 1945:
The first trial of accused German war criminals begins in Nuremberg, Germany.

January 24, 1946:
The Atomic Energy Commission is formed to monitor the development of nuclear energy and weapons.

June 14, 1947:
On the seventh anniversary of the arrival of the camp's first prisoners, the Auschwitz-Birkenau Memorial and Museum opens its first permanent exhibition.

Remembering

As the years passed after the war, civic groups across the globe came forward to establish memorials and places of remembrance for soldiers and civilians who had sacrificed so much and to ensure that the devastation of the Second World War would never be repeated. Even in the midst of the war, the United States began to establish military cemeteries in foreign lands. Overlooking Omaha Beach, the Normandy American Cemetery and Memorial became the first U.S. cemetery on European soil in World War II, with the initial site constructed only two days after D-Day. One of fourteen U.S. military cemeteries in foreign territory, the cemetery contains the remains of 9,387 Americans who died during the invasion of France.

In addition to honoring soldiers who died in battle, memorials remember the millions of civilians who died during the war. The United States Holocaust Memorial Museum in Washington, D.C., is dedicated to serving "as this country's memorial to the millions of people murdered during the Holocaust." In Europe, several concentration camps have been converted into public memorials, including Auschwitz-Birkenau, Buchenwald, and Dachau.

In Japan, the Hiroshima Peace Memorial Museum was established at ground zero, the site of the atomic bombing of August 6, 1945. Established ten years after the war, the museum continues to advocate for the dis-

mantling of all nuclear weapons.

In the hopes of remembering the innumerable sacrifices of the war, and to create a national memorial during the lifetimes of the remaining World War II veterans, the American Battle Monuments Commission created the National World War II Memorial on the Mall in Washington, D.C. The memorial's opening on April 29, 2004, followed more than ten years of planning, with public fundraising donating more than $150 million for the project. As the number of people who experienced the conflict's many triumphs and tragedies declines year by year, these memorials serve as timeless witnesses of the war's history for future generations. ✪

"Because I remember, I despair. Because I remember, I have the duty to reject despair."

—Elie Wiesel, Holocaust survivor, 1986

April 3, 1948:
President Truman approves the Marshall Plan, providing funds for the rebuilding of post-war Europe.

April 4, 1949:
The United States, Canada, and several Western European nations sign the North Atlantic Treaty, which creates the North Atlantic Treaty Organization (NATO).

September 8, 1951:
Prepared by the U.S. and Britain, the Japanese Peace Treaty is signed by forty-nine nations in San Francisco, California.

GLOSSARY

Allies: Coalition of nations that included the Soviet Union, Great Britain, the United States, Poland, France, and China, among others.

Amphibious: Assault strategy in which forces arrived by sea to make a land invasion.

Axis: Wartime alliance principally between Germany, Italy, and Japan.

The Blitz: German air raids over London and other cities in England.

Blitzkrieg: "Lightning war." Fast, overwhelming use of force by the German military.

Civil defense: Programs to protect the home front against enemy attacks.

Concentration camps: Initially, Nazi prisons for political opponents. Later became death camps operated to exterminate Jews and other groups.

D-Day: June 6, 1944. Day of the Allied invasion of Normandy, France.

Decrypt: To decode an encrypted message.

Einsatzgruppen: Nazi mobile killing squads.

Encrypt: To take a message and make it secret using a private code

Enigma: German encryption machine.

Espionage: Spying.

Internment: Imprisonment of people of Japanese descent within the United States.

Kamikaze: "Divine wind." Japanese suicide fighter planes.

League of Nations: The predecessor to the United Nations; created after World War I.

Luftwaffe: German Air Force.

Magic: U.S. code name for Japanese diplomatic code.

Manhattan Project: U.S. program to develop the atomic bomb.

Operation Barbarossa: The Axis invasion of the Soviet Union.

Operation Overlord: The Allied invasion of Axis-occupied France.

Panzer: German tank.

POW: Prisoner of war.

Purple: Japanese diplomatic encryption machine.

Rationing: Using less of an item in order to maintain supplies.

Reichstag: Prewar German parliament.

Theater (ie. Pacific Theater): Region of the war.

Trinity Test: Successful atomic bomb test in New Mexico on July 16, 1945.

V-E Day: May 8, 1945. Victory in Europe Day.

V-J Day: August 15, 1945. Victory over Japan Day.

Wehrmacht: German armed forces.

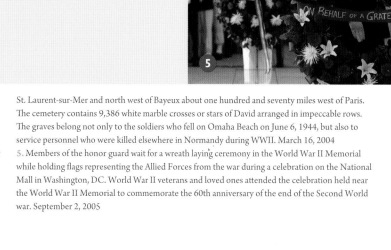

1. President Truman attends the burial of twenty soldiers at Arlington National Cemetery. These twenty were the first who died and were returned to be buried in their native land. October 30, 1947
2. President Reagan gives a speech on the 40th Anniversary of D-Day at Pointe du Hoc, Normandy, France. June 16, 1984
3. 63rd anniversary of the Hiroshima bomb: Candles and paper lanterns float on the Motoyasu River in front of the Atomic Bomb Dome, in memory of the victims of the Hiroshima bomb. Peace Memorial Park, Hiroshima, Japan. August 6, 2008
4. The World War II Normandy American Cemetery and Memorial, which is situated on a cliff overlooking Omaha Beach and the English Channel in Colleville-sur Mer, France. It is just east of St. Laurent-sur-Mer and north west of Bayeux about one hundred and seventy miles west of Paris. The cemetery contains 9,386 white marble crosses or stars of David arranged in impeccable rows. The graves belong not only to the soldiers who fell on Omaha Beach on June 6, 1944, but also to service personnel who were killed elsewhere in Normandy during WWII. March 16, 2004
5. Members of the honor guard wait for a wreath laying ceremony in the World War II Memorial while holding flags representing the Allied Forces from the war during a celebration on the National Mall in Washington, DC. World War II veterans and loved ones attended the celebration held near the World War II Memorial to commemorate the 60th anniversary of the end of the Second World war. September 2, 2005

EUROPE, 1945
MAJOR OPERATIONS OF WORLD WAR TWO

0 100 200 300 400
SCALE OF MILES

NORWAY

Oslo ★

NORTH
SEA

DENMARK
Copenhagen ★

IRELAND

GREAT BRITAIN

Amsterdam
NETHERLANDS

Hamburg

Berlin

London ★
EISENHOWER

BELGIUM

GERMANY

Von Rundstedt
(Dec. 1944-Jan. 1945)

Torgau

English Channel

MONTGOMERY
(Aug. 1944-May 1945)

Remagen

Normandy Invasion,
D-Day, 6 June 1944

(June 1944)

BRADLEY
(Aug. 1944-
May 1945)

Paris ★

Battle of the Bulge

Prague ★

CZE

ATLANTIC OCEAN

FRANCE

DEVERS
(Sept. 1944-
May 1945)

Munich

Vi

AUSTR

Vichy ○

SWITZERLAND

ALPS MOUNTAINS

Trieste

Lyons ○

CLARK
(Jan.-May 1945)

PATCH
(Aug.-Sept. 1944)

PYRENEES MTNS.

ANDORRA

St. Tropez, 1944

Po River

ADRIATIC

PORTUGAL

CORSICA

ITALY

Madrid ★

Rome ★

Anzio, 1943

SPAIN

SARDINIA

Naples ○

Sa

From Great Britain

From U.S.
PATTON (Nov. 1942)

Gibraltar
(Great Britain)

RYDER
(Nov. 1942)

ALEXANDER
(Nov. 1942-May 1943)

Palermo

Mazagan

Port Lyautey

SPANISH MOROCCO
(SPAIN)

Oran ○

Algiers ★

Bizerte

Tunis, 1944

Casablanca ○

Bône ○

Sicily Invasion, 1943

Safi ○

FREDENALL
(Nov. 1942)

Kasserine Pass, 1943

MALTA
(GREAT BRITAIN)

MOROCCO
(FRANCE)

ALGERIA
(FRANCE)

TUNISIA
(FRANCE)

MED I

Mareth, 1943

Tripoli ★

○ City or Town

⊛ National Capital

National Boundaries

Battle Site

Axis Advance

Allied Advance (American & British)

Allied Advance (Soviet)

Allies

Axis

Neutral Countries

Axis Controlled (Max. Extent)

LIB
(ITA

FINLAND

★ Helsinki
○ Leningrad
★ Stockholm

(Jan.-Dec. 1944)

ESTONIA

BALTIC SEA

L A T V I A

Riga ★

Memel ○ LITHUANIA

Smolensk

(June 1944-Feb. 1945)

S O V I E T   U N I O N

EAST
PRUSSIA
(GER.)

○nzig
(ansk)

Minsk ○

Gomel ○

☆ Kursk, 1943

Vistula

Warsaw ○ Brest (July 1943-Dec. 1944)

May 1945)

★ ○

P O L A N D

(July 1943-June 1944)

Kharkov ○

Kiev ○

(June 1944-May 1945)

○weitz ○

Lvov ○

CARPATHIAN MOUNTAINS

VAKIA

●pest ★

NGARY

ROMANIA

(June 1944-May 1945)

Sevastopol ○

Yalta ○

(June 1944-May 1945)

Belgrade ★

Bucharest ★

B L A C K   S E A

GOSLAVIA

Danube   River

BULGARIA

Sofia ★

ALBANIA

Istanbul ○

T U R K E Y

GREECE

AEGEAN
SEA

DODECANESE ISLAND
(ITALY)

CYPRUS
(GREAT BRITAIN)

CRETE

ANEAN   SEA

Benghazi ○

☆ Tobruk, 1942

Cairo ★

E G Y P T

Nile River

RED
SEA

Major operations of
World War II. Europe, 1945